Seasons

Coming Soon by Tina Melson

Secrets

Sacrifices

Seasons

A Christian Love Story

Tina Melson

the Butterfly Typeface

Books published by **The Butterfly Typeface Publishing** may be purchased for educational, business or sales promotional use. For information please write: Attn: Iris M Williams, *The Butterfly Typeface Publishing*, PO Box 56193, Little Rock, AR 72215.

First Edition

ISBN: 978-1-942022-12-1

"I can do all things through Christ which strengthen me."

Philippians 4:13

Dedication

I dedicate this book to Abraham Harris because without his encouragement I would never have picked up my pen and finished this book. He encouraged me to dig deep inside myself, pull my dreams off the shelf and make them a reality.

Acknowledgments

I thank God first and foremost for allowing me to have the mindset and the patience to sit down and tell stories that can be heard. God gave me a vision many years ago and told me if I plant seeds they will grow.

I've planted so many seeds in the ground for this harvest. I've pulled up so many weeds that sometimes I thought I had sown on fallow/ hollow grounds!

Thanks be to God that some fell on good soil and my vision is beginning to grow. I give God all the praise!

He set me on a mission and without putting Latrea Wyche in my path, I never would have met Iris M. Williams and for these two beautiful angels, I give God the glory!

Tina Melson

Seasons

Eight Months Earlier...

D wayne and I would always get together after choir rehearsal and meet at his condo. We always ended up in bed making love until the break of day. Who would have thought this man wouldn't eventually be my husband?

I had a vision of walking down the aisle at MT. Nebo with everyone in attendance. Heck, I had even picked out my bridesmaids. My best friend Jackie would be my maid of honor and even Deacon James Wilson, (Pastor Ron Willis' best friend) was all ready to walk me down the aisle.

Everything was going great, according to me. I always thought with my heart and felt as if other people did also. I never had a 'what if' enter my thoughts. If Dwayne and I were lying here making love, then in my mind we were already married. Now eight months later, there is no marriage and no Dwayne. All hope is lost.

Nicki continued to think and she remembered something her mom used to say.

We live by seasons. Mother Christine would say.

If that was true, then this was supposed to be the season for happiness for her and Dwayne. Nicki wondered.

What went wrong in this season? She had no idea.

Nicki thought that this season had ended, but in fact it was only the beginning! God has a plan and purpose for our lives. **Luke 21** reads, "Watch ye therefore and pray always that you may be counted worthy to escape all these things that shall come to pass and to stand before the son of man." Nicki was passing through the fiery furnace. She had to weather this storm. God's glory was right there in the middle, right there in her tears, right there in her fears, right there in her draught ... right there in the middle of her life.

Walk in His Glory

Nicki Williams wondered for the thirteenth time how she could be so dumb to do what she told herself that she would never do again. Why did she keep giving her heart and body to men when she knew in her heart that it would always end the same way?

As she sat looking out her bedroom window thinking how messed up her life was, the phone rang. Looking at the caller Id, she recognized her best friend's number.

Hi Jackie. What's up?

Jackie knew right away that Nicki's tone was off and that something was bothering her.

Hey, I'm on my way over and I'll pick up dinner. I just need to relax and chill with my BFF for a little while.

A short while later, Jackie and I were eating and talking.

So tell me what's really going on with you and Dwayne.

I looked across the table at my best friend and knew that I could talk to her about anything so I began to tell her how I let Dwayne into my heart and into my bed and how things began to go downhill pretty fast:

I thought that because he was so good to me and was saying all the right things that he would propose to me and all the time it ended up all about sex. This time I'm not so sure that I'll be able to bounce back. I know what Pastor Willis has been teaching us and I just got so caught up with what Dwayne was doing for me that I thought it only right that I should share everything with him. I messed up.

I knew that Jackie was a virgin and still waiting on Mr. Right. Jackie took my hand and led me over to the couch and after we were seated she began to pray:

Dear heavenly Father we come to you as humbly as we know how, first of all thanking you for your sweet son Jesus who died on Calvary for our sins, Lord we are asking for forgiveness for our trespasses and our sins we ask that do come into our hearts and make us whole again we ask that you restore us and bless us to be what you require us to be. Lord we will be so careful to give you all honor and glory in your sweet son name we pray. Amen.

After she finished praying she looked into my eyes and said, "*God has forgiven you. Now you forgive yourself and walk in His glory.*"

Jackie always knew what to do in any situation. We talked for a little while longer then she left. After Jackie left I showered and went to bed.

The Best for You

Day light came quickly. I worked as a social worker in the city of Jacksonville. As I was driving into work, traffic was slow so my mind began to wonder back at the time when I first met Dwayne.

Dwayne was not what you would call good looking, but what really caught my eye was that he was always willing to help anybody in need. We met at church. Dwayne was the youth leader and I sang in the choir. Every Sunday he would look over at me and wink. In the beginning I thought that he had a facial tic because he winked that one eye all the time. In time I knew that wink was for me.

One night after practice he stopped me as I was getting in my car and asked me out to coffee and I accepted. That turned out to be a great night. We talked about everything: friends, family and most of all God. I remember him telling me that he was saved and I thought how rare to hear a man confess to being saved. So I listen to every word that he said. I remember praying and asking God to send me a man that loved Him so that he could surely love me. I took that as a good sign from God.

Looking back on that night now I realize that that was the beginning of his game. Oh I know that I can't blame him for everything but right now I am sure going to try.

A car horn sounded behind me and brought me back to present. Enough with the daydreaming, time to get to work. I made a mental note to stop at my sister's house that evening after work and see my new niece. I then headed into work.

The day went by pretty fast and before I knew it, it was time to go. My sister and her husband lived in a beautiful house in a new subdivision right off of interstate 91. As I was turning into the subdivision I thought of how hard my brother-in-law worked to make sure his family had everything that they needed.

When Ryan found out that Monica was having their baby he took on an extra job so that by the time the baby was born they would have a home instead of the apartment they were living in. Ryan's a deacon at Mt. Nebo where my family attends church. Monica was a secretary at the church and they met, fell madly in love and within the year the two were planning a wedding! Monica swore that she would be a virgin until she was married. I don't know but I do know that Ryan was so in love with her that he would do anything for her before the marriage and now he seemed even more in love with her even after being married three years.

Monica was standing at the door when I got out of my car. I hugged her as I stepped inside the foyer. Her house was beautifully decorated and before I could ask about my niece, I heard baby sounds coming from the den. She had gotten so big since I last saw her. I picked her up and gave her a big kiss. Alesia laughed with delight.

After playing with the baby for a while I put her back in her play pen and followed the good smell that was coming out of the kitchen. Monica was a great cook and tonight she was cooking my favorite - chicken. I grabbed a piece and began chewing on it. Monica gave me the look and I grinned back at her.

You haven't changed a bit you know. How are things going with you and Dwayne? Are you guys ready to plan a wedding yet.

I knew it would make no sense to lie to her so I told her the truth.

Dwayne and I are finished. I don't know why I can't seem to keep a man in my life. I don't know what I'm doing wrong.

I think you need to go talk to mom.

You know mom and I always clash when it comes down to my life.

What I know is that you cannot accept that mom knows best.

When she finds out that Dwayne and I are no longer together she's going to go into that preaching mode and say, "Before you make any decisions you should talk to God and He will direct your steps."

What's wrong with that? Monica asked. *Mom has always given me great advice and my life has turned out alright.*

I know, you were always her favorite.

Now you are tripping. We both were her favorite.

I guess, but sometimes I thought she was too hard on me.

She only wants the best for you, you do know that. Monica assured.

Yea I guess you're right. Maybe I'll stop by after church on Sunday.

Let Him Use You

After leaving Monica's, I stopped by the church for choir practice and dreaded to go in because I knew that I would run into Dwayne. On Wednesday he always stayed late because Pastor Willis met with all the church leaders.

As I sat in the car I sent a quick prayer up to God asking that I wouldn't run into him tonight. My mind began to wonder back down memory lane and I thought about the good times Dwayne and I had together. I remembered he had dark skin that looked like Hershey candy and was just as smooth, eyes so brown that you could lose your way looking in them and lips so luscious that when you kissed them you never wanted to stop. Dwayne had a smile that could melt any sane person's heart. I could not wait for him to meet my parents. I just knew that because he was active in the church my parents would love him as much as I did.

I gave myself a little shake and brought myself back from daydreaming. As I entered the church the choir was warming up. I took my place and began to sing like I had never sung before. Everybody was looking at me like I had just received the best actress award.

"Darn girl what has gotten into you," Dasha the choir director asked me. *"You singing like you are up for an award. I have been trying to get you to sing like that for years!"*

Everybody started clapping and a few choir members had tears in their eyes. I was as amazed as they were I didn't know where it came from. Pastor Willis and Dwayne were standing in the doorway when I looked up. Pastor Willis came over to me, looked in my eyes and ask me if I was Nicki or Christine, my mom.

My mom used to play and sing with the choir before she retired. She loved the Lord with all her heart and she didn't compromise her position for anybody.

I told Pastor Willis that I didn't know what came over me. He just shook his head and said, "Just keep on letting God use you."

Use me? How was God using *me* when I had been doing any and everything? I wondered but did not voice it out loud.

Dwayne just walked away. I wanted so badly to say something to him but I was too afraid.

He's Working on You Daily

I went home, fixed a snack and called my mom. She answered on the first ring as though she was expecting me to call.

Hey baby, how are you?

I'm fine and you?

I'm fine too. Monica told me that you dropped by today.

Yes I wanted to see my niece. She has gotten so big and those big brown eyes are adorable.

I know ... my first grandchild. Tell me what's going on in your world.

I didn't call to talk about me, how are you?

Look child I know something is bothering you, Pastor Willis stopped by tonight for a cup of coffee and told me that you sung your little heart out at rehearsal tonight. Baby God's throne is always accessible to His children.

My mom had a way of adding wisdom and religion to any conversation she and I had. For years now I always suspected that she and the good Pastor was seeing each other so just to get on her nerves I had to tease her.

Is coffee the only thing Pastor came for?

I am not going to entertain that devil in you tonight so if you need to say something say it now before I hang up on you.

Ok mom I was just kidding, I called to tell you I'll be home for Sunday dinner.

My mom always cooked Sunday dinner and usually her table was full of family and friends on Sunday evening. She started doing this way before I was born and has made it a tradition. Everybody knew that you could always come to Mother Christine's on Sunday.

Mom do you think I could come early and we could have a talk?

You didn't have to ask you know you can. Do you need to come now?

No Sunday will be ok, it's the Lord's Day and I'll let Him do his work.

Child, every day is the Lords' day and He's working on you daily.
Ok mom I'll see you Sunday.

When I hung up the phone I thought about Pastor Willis and how he seemed to be at mom's house a lot. I know that she's a beautiful woman and since my dad died twelve years ago Pastor Willis has been there for her.

His wife had passed two years before my dad and they seem to have formed a special bond that I needed to come to terms with. Don't get me wrong I like my Pastor I just don't think I need a step dad now. I want my mom to be happy but I'm not sure if she knows what she's doing. Look at me calling the pot black. It's strange how I can give advice but can't take any.

I remember my mom just staring at me as if I'd grown two heads when I informed her that I was going to drop out of school and marry my then boyfriend Gary. Gary was special and when I say special I don't mean unique. She just let me go on thinking that I knew it all.

Gary didn't last and neither did Ronald or any of the others I had brought home over the years.

Wisdom

After church on Sunday I rushed over to moms before anyone else arrived. I needed to talk to her without anyone being around. My mom was not big on fireworks, which I always brought to the table when she and I talked. She was however big on prayer, quietly watching, patiently waiting and desperately counting on God to help her deal with me.

She believed that wisdom was knowing what's right then saying the right things at the right time for the right reason. By that definition my mother was a very wise woman especially when it came to the boys and men I dated.

When I walked thru the door she took one look at me and led me to the den.

Before you say anything I just want you to know that I love you and whatever you are going through, this too will pass.

I hugged her so tight and I began to cry.

Mom all my life I have been messing up in love. God must not want me to have a husband or give you grandbabies.

Baby, that's not true. God wants you to be happy but right now your focus should be on you not a man. Sometimes you have to know how to wait on the Lord not on man. How can you make someone else happy and you are not happy with yourself? Concentrate on you Nicki and everything else will fall in place. Dry your eyes now and come help me in the kitchen.

Mom had a way of turning everything around. As we entered the kitchen the doorbell rang.

I'll get it mom go on and finish in the kitchen.

Opening the door I thought about everything my mom had said and decided I would just enjoy the evening.

Pastor Willis was the first to arrive and after I greeted him, I saw my sister and her family were coming up the walkway. After every one got there the house was so full. People were everywhere talking, laughing and just having a great time, because of course nobody can cook the way mama can.

After dinner Pastor Willis said that he had an announcement to make. He grabbed moms hand and brought it to his lips, looked into her eyes and smiled. Mom gave a slight nod, her eyes never leaving his and then he looked at everyone there and made his announcement.

Christine has agreed to make me the happiest man alive and be my wife.

At first everyone looked shocked and then cheers went up all around the room. Mom came over where Monica and I stood and gave us both big hugs.

I hope you girls are not too shocked by Ron's announcement but he wanted to tell our family and friends together and what better way than Sunday dinner.

I was still standing with my mouth hanging open looking crazy. Monica reached up and gave my mom another hug and kissed her on the cheek.

I'm so happy for you mom. I know Pastor Willis will be a wonderful husband.

The only thing going thru my mind was that my mom had found a husband before I had.

Brokenness Be Restored

W hat did I do to God for Him to play such a cruel joke on me? I couldn't even think straight. I needed some fresh air so I headed outside, but before I could reach the door Pastor Willis grabbed my hand and led me into the den. I wanted to snatch my hand away but I didn't.

As we stood facing each other I suddenly burst out crying. Pastor Willis pulled me into his arms and started saying comforting and soothing words to me. Jackie knocked on the door and stuck her head in but he waved her away.

I'm sorry I didn't mean to cry. This just caught me off guard.

He just looked and me and smiled and after a few minutes he suggested that we pray.

Father helps us to understand those things even when our understanding is limited. Help us to live for you Lord. Speak a word Lord, show us the plans you have for us. Bind us to your word and strengthen us so that we have

the courage to forgive and to accept forgiveness. May our brokenness be restored for the beauty of your glory? Please help us to except your plan and grace, in Jesus name we pray. Amen.

I looked at my Pastor, soon to be stepfather, and saw the glory of the Lord in his face. I knew that my mom deserved this good man standing before me and I understood his love for me. He had seen me as a child and watched me grow into a woman and I knew that he wanted me to be all that I could be.

I just didn't know how to be the woman that he saw. I looked at him and threw my arms around him and told him to first forgive me for being so selfish then forgive me for my outburst and the tears. I told him that it was an honor and a privilege to be his stepdaughter.

He smiled and then he kissed me on the cheek and told me that if I ever needed to talk about anything that he would always be there to listen.

As we joined the others Pastor gave me a wink. Jackie walked over to me and asked was I ok and I said yes.

During the night I woke up and couldn't get back to sleep so I got up, went to my window seat and looked up at the stars and thought back to the time in my life that I thought I was happy. I thought Dwayne was the answer to my prayers. He was charming, witty and oh so handsome to me. He came into my life like he was my shining knight. We talked so much about our dreams and our future. He told me about his family, his mom and dad how they had been married thirty years and was still so much in love with each other as the day they married.

Dwayne has one brother who is a minister and a sister who teaches school. His family is his life. They get together once a week to catch up on each other's life and to see if help is needed anywhere. I used to love the weekly gatherings. His dad would always start out with prayer. I knew that I would be Dwayne's wife one day. We were so happy I thought.

For over a year I lived, breath, and knew only Dwayne. I guess that's where I went wrong, I forgot about me and what makes me happy. I just wanted him to be happy.

I remember one time I was on my way to choir practice and as I came into the church parking lot I saw Dwayne opening the car door for Dasha to get out and I saw him whisper something in her ear and they both laughed and walked inside the church. I thought it strange but later that night after practice he was waiting for me just like he had been doing from the beginning of our relationship so I didn't mention it and soon forgot it.

Then another time Monica and I had lunch at O'Charleys and we spotted Dasha and Dwayne having lunch. Monica and I stopped by their table on the way out and he got up and kissed me like nothing was going on. On the phone that night he explained it as church business. I knew from time to time he and Dasha had meetings about the youth plays and many productions the church put on. So I felt I had no need to worry.

I had made Dwayne my 'everything' and that's why my world was turned upside down now that I didn't have him.

Dwayne and Dasha were to be married in less than two months. I thought about going to the wedding but I knew that I couldn't go. Who wants to see the man of their dreams marry another woman?

Then I thought maybe I would be a good person and send them a very nice wedding gift and with that in mind I got back into bed and slept like a log.

Out in the Open

Morning can too soon and before I knew it I was up getting dressed and headed to work. The day turned out beautiful and after work I decided to do a little shopping. I stopped by the mall, bought a really nice outfit and shoes to match.

On the way home I called Jackie because she gets off work two hours after I do.

Hey girl how was your day?

Who is this?

It's me silly.

I thought so but I haven't heard you sound so cheerful in so long I thought I was talking to another person.

No it's me and I'm feeling so good today I thought maybe you'd like to meet me for a bite to eat.

Ok where you want to go?

There is a new place that I've been dying to eat at, it's called Dugan's. I heard that they have the best seafood in town.

Ok see you in twenty minutes.

As I parked the car I gave God a private high five for letting me be able to let Dwayne go. In my mind or should I say my private thoughts I knew or thought I knew that one day we would get back together again. That was why I could smile and pretend that everything was going to be alright in my world.

Jackie arrived, we went inside the restaurant and after the waiter seated us Jackie got down to business.

Nicki you know that I love you girl and I only want the best for you. I know that you are planning something in that head of yours and I'm here to tell you that it won't work.

I pretended to not understand her because I was thinking who she to give me advice was. Instead I looked her straight in the eyes and denied everything she said.

Girl really I'm fine with Dwayne and Dasha. I was even thinking about buying a gift for them.

Jackie looked at me as though I had grown another head. *You cannot be serious don't go entertaining that idea. You know that if you play with fire you get burned.*

Who said I was playing.

Look Nicki let sleeping dogs lie it is the best thing you can do right now.

Even though Jackie was right I just could not let Dwayne go in my heart that easy.

Ok I'll leave this alone for now.

Jackie gave me one last mean look before she changed the subject.

So how's your mom wedding plans coming along?

We are going to look at wedding dresses on Saturday it's the only time Monica can leave the baby with Ryan. Do you want to come with us?

No I promised some of my co-workers I would help out with this year's food drive.

Ok. Seriously, Jackie do you think that it's over between Dwayne and I?

I think that when God closes a door it should stay closed. He cheated on you and he broke your heart and you still feel some kind of good way toward him. Don't you know that if he loved you that would have never happened? Nicki, I pray that God will open your spiritual eye so that you can see him for who he really is.

Thank you for being a real friend to me. I'm going to think about this for a while.

It's out in the open now. Let's just enjoying this meal and each other's company.

Closed Doors

A fter I got home and was relaxing in the tub my phone began to ring. I closed my eyes and thought to myself I'll call who ever that's calling me back.

I thought about walking up in that church and telling Dwayne that I'm the girl that he's supposed to be marrying. I'm the one who really loves him. I should be his wife not Dasha.

While my thoughts were getting the best of me my phone was ringing off the hook.

Hello?

It was Pastor Willis.

I called to see if maybe you can meet me for dinner tomorrow. I think we need to talk.

I tried to think of something, anything and I couldn't come up with a reason why not. I agreed to meet him around seven for dinner.

My phone rang again. This time it was Monica checking up on me like when we were children. Monica was an overly protective sister. She was mature and loved to be in charge of everything. I could always depend on her to do what was best for the both of us.

So Nic (that's what she always called me when she was about to have a serious conversation with me), *you know that I know that things have not been working out the way that you thought they would especially between you and Dwayne. I know you think that he was the best thing for you. But as you know when God decides to close a door in your life it's best to leave that door closed. I know that mind of yours is thinking up ways to get him back but I want you to leave that door closed. So what, he hurt you. I think that you are more embarrassed than hurt. I know that there were signs in the relationship that you saw but ignored. And if you looked back over the time you two spent together you will see that he never treated you like you deserved to be treated. I know that he was charming, good-looking, and versed in the bible, but the devil knows scripture too. Nic everything that glitters ain't gold and everything that shines ain't silver. That's what granny use to say. When I met Ryan he treated me as if I would break. He never required me to be anything or anyone other than myself. He would however, challenge me to be better. He loved me sometimes more than I loved myself and encouraged me when I thought I had nothing left to give. Never once did Ryan over step any boundary. He didn't come looking to take but he came to restore. That's when you know that its God ordained. Nic you know the bible and what it says about being equally yoked. Don't let the devil take your joy away from you. I once heard a speaker say that many people will reach their destination but not their destiny. I want you to find your way through this. I know that God's favor is on your life. Favor can do for you what nothing else can do. Baby girl right now you are not walking in your destiny. Understand who you are. Things don't move you, you move things! Nic, you need to find yourself before you lose yourself. I love you and I want the best for you. Do you believe that?*

Yes I believe that. You've given me some things to think about. Monica I love you, thank you for your insight and your wisdom. I needed someone to tell me that what I was thinking about doing was wrong. Monica he hurt me so bad. All the while we were dating he talked about God as though he had a personal relationship with Him. I believed everything he said to me, every lie he told me. I even gave him what I knew I shouldn't have. I was in love and this hurts like crazy.

I began to cry uncontrollably. Monica was trying to comfort me but to no avail. The more she tried to soothe me the more I cried. All the hurt, anger, and frustration of the past few months came out.

Finally I was able to calm down enough to say good-bye to Monica. I don't know how long I sat there, because I couldn't bring myself to move off of the sofa and get in bed. I just pulled the throw over me and slept right there on the couch.

Lifting Spirits

Morning came and I was awakened by my cell ringing. I looked at the clock and it was past eleven. My first instinct was not to answer but whoever on the other end of my cell were not giving up that easy.

Hello?

It was Jackie.

Hey girl. Are we going to shop today or not it's already eleven and I haven't heard from you? All the girls are waiting at the mall.

The girls were Erika, Bea, and Janea. Once a month we all got together for shopping and a little girl bonding time. By bonding I mean gossiping, laughing a lot and having fun. Always on these outings everybody really enjoy themselves.

I'm getting dressed now and I'll meet you there.

At the mall, we shopped 'til we almost dropped. Erika suggested that we get a bite to eat. We all knew that if we went shopping Erika would be the first to want to get something to eat. Since Frances, a popular eatery, is in the mall we agreed to go there. We quickly found a big table at the back so we wouldn't disturb the few early customers. As soon as we were seated, Bea the more serious one of our group told us to hold hands and she began to pray.

Lord, enlarge our territory, bless us indeed. Let your hand be with us and keep us from all evil. Bless this food and bless the preparers in the mighty name of Jesus. Amen.

We all followed with Amen.

After the waitress took our food and drink orders, Janea started running her mouth as usual.

I heard that Dwayne dumped you for Dasha. I couldn't believe you didn't call me!

In response, I looked at her and rolled my eyes. I didn't want to talk about Dwayne, but I knew she wasn't going to let it go.

He didn't dump me, we both decided to see other people, I responded.
You might as well come clean Nicki. You know that we love you and we have your back, Janea said with disbelief.

I just gave her that whatever look.

Once again, Jackie spoke up and took it upon herself to catch everyone up on my situation because she knew that if I told the story I would end up in tears.

Look everyone, Jackie began. *Nicki and Dwayne have broken up. He was cheating with Dasha.*

Let's go open up a can of whoop ass on her, Janae said.

I looked at Janea who was *always* ready to fight.

For what? Dwayne knows who he wants and he wants Dasha. I've moved on so let's just talk about something else, I said desperately trying to change the subject.

Bea, the philosophical one of the group, spoke up. *Girl you've got to know your purpose, then you have to make plans and prepare, then go out and produce. You don't need a man in your life to make or break you. We love you anyway.*

The four of us has been friends since kindergarten and if one hurt we all hurt.

Then Janea spoke again, *do you all remember when we were in the eighth grade and we all had this huge crush on Daniel?*

We all cracked up laughing because we remembered that. Daniel had been so confused because he knew he couldn't date one without dating us all.

Yea he knew that we stuck together like glue, Bea said. *Guess after all these years he finally made a choice.*

How so, I asked.

Because he chose me, Bea replied.

We all looked at her.

Don't look so confused, Bea said. *What I mean is that I've been seeing him for a while now.*

No way, I said.

We all started laughing and asking questions at the same time.
Nobody knew you were seeing him! How did you keep this to yourself? I continued.

Erika knew, Bea informed us.

We all looked at Erika then.

What, Erika cried in self-defense. *She didn't want me to tell you guys because she didn't know where the relationship was headed.*

Wow, I said. *We are so out of touch with each other that we are keeping secrets from everyone?*

Bea responded slowly, *Nicki you have been so busy with Dwayne that you never get together with us anymore. And Janea you have been in hiding for a while too. Every time I call you, you're. Anyway, now that we're all here I have something to tell all of you. Daniel asked me to marry him and I said yes!*

She shrieked and started waving her finger to show off her diamond engagement ring. We all jumped up and started hugging her. After we were all once again seated, Bea continued to talk.

We've been trying to avoid having 'you-know-what' for a while because you all know that Pastor Willis speaks against having sex before marriage. Ladies when I tell you that's a hard thing to do believe me it is. You know at bible study Wednesday night, Pastor taught on how it is better to be married than to burn in eternity. He asked the question, "Shall we continue in sin that grace shall abound?" Daniel and I both love the Lord too much to continue in sin. Sometimes we love so hard that we forget that sex before marriage is sin. We made a vow that night that if we love the Lord and each other then we would be married to each other and make God happy.

Janea spoke up then and said, *it's amazing how you can pour yourself into people that doesn't pour themselves into you.*

How so, Bea asked her.

My love has been given freely even when there was no benefit, Janea responded.

What in the world are you talking about, we all asked in unison.

Last year I started going out with Sherman's uncle Dale. It started out good but it went downhill a few months ago. I wanted marriage and he didn't. He's not getting any younger you know, she said sarcastically. *Well I talked about it every time we got together. At first he did too, but then he started avoiding the subject and soon stopped talking about it all together. I think he's seeing someone else so I broke it off. He hasn't called once. I'm so hurt because we were lovers. Yes, you all heard me right, we were making love. I don't think that there are men out here dating women that they don't sleep with. He noticed me asked me out and yes ladies we've been busy.*

Erika quickly chimed in. *He stopped seeing you because you worried the man so much about marriage. Maybe he has a hang up about it. Maybe he's waiting on God. I know that you are a hand full and you don't take any mess, so maybe you were just too much for him. Girl you need to slow down on acting like you're still twenty instead of thirty something. Love will find you.*

Like it has found you? Janea said obviously getting upset.

I knew that the conversation was getting heated so I stepped in and quickly changed the subject by asking Bea about her plans for her wedding?

I want all of you in my wedding, Bea said happily. *I've just now decided who will be my matron of honor.* She turned to look at Janea. *Janea will you be my matron of honor? Yes I will*, Janea said with excitement, *but why me?*

Bea didn't miss a beat. *I think that this would be the perfect opportunity for Dale to see you as the beautiful woman that you are. The rest of you will be my bridesmaids. Now let's talk wedding!*

Before I knew it, it was five o' clock and I had promised the good Rev. that I would meet him for dinner at seven.

Ladies I really enjoyed myself but I have to go or I'll be late for my date.

Everybody gave me that '*What date*' look before busting out laughing. I gave them my serious look and said, *Oh I can't have a date?*

In unison they all replied, *No!*

We all laughed.

I had a good time. I said as I stood to leave. *You guy's always know how to lift a girls spirit up, but I really do have a dinner date at seven. I'll call you all later tonight and let you all know how it went.*

As I turned to leave, I glanced back at them and the look on their faces was priceless. *Serves them right for teasing me*, I thought with a smile.

He's Not For You

I went home, took a shower and changed into a comfortable shirt and skirt. I arrived at the restaurant just as Pastor Ron was getting out of his car. We walked inside together. After we were seated Ron asked what I would like to eat. I let him order for me. While he ordered I wondered what he wanted to talk to me about. I was praying that he wanted to talk about mom and their wedding. While I was thinking on what he was going to say, he suddenly asked me,

If you were to die today (God forbid) what would you want your loved ones to say about you?

That question took me by surprise. I looked at him and asked, *what?*

He repeated the question and said, "*Be honest with your self would you want them to lie about you or not say anything at all.*"

I thought about it and decided I'd want them to be honest.

If someone said something about me now it wouldn't sound so good would it?
Instead of answering the question he said,

Nicki, women have been pleasing men since the beginning of times. In **Mark Chapter 6 Verse22** *it says*, "The daughter of said Herodias came in and danced it pleased Herod and he told her to ask whatever and he would give it to her, even half of his kingdom." *What I'm asking you baby girl is what do you want your loved ones to say about you.*

I want people to say, "She loved the Lord with all her heart." I answered. *And that, "She was obedient."*

Then child if you want your loved ones to respect you and talk good about you know that in the beginning of creation God made them male and female. **Mark Chapter 10, verses 6-9** *says*, "For this cause man shall leave his mother and father and cleave to his wife and they twain shall be one flesh. What God hath joined together, let no man put asunder?" *I know Monica talked to you last night and I just wanted to let you know just how much your family loves you and want the best for you. I'm not saying Dwayne is not a good man, I'm saying he's not for you. It's done the relationship is over and God has a bigger plan for your life. I know it seems hard now but it gets easier and easier as time goes by. Just you wait and see. God is trying to use you for His glory. I know you don't get that but keep praying and watch Him work things out in your favor. You are highly favored my child and don't let anyone tell you differently.*

This brought tears to my eyes. As I wiped them away I decided that I had shed my last tear for Dwayne and I wouldn't waste anymore sleep over him. I was moving on with my life. I needed a wake- up call and my soon to be step dad and my sister opened up my eyes.

After dinner Pastor Ron took a tiny box out of his coat pocket and gave it to me. I looked at it and he said, *go on open it, it's for you.*

Inside was the most beautiful pendant I had ever seen. I got up, hugged him and kissed him on the cheek.

Thank you so much it's gorgeous, I love it.

Deliverance

A fter I left the restaurant I rode by the church. As I pulled in the parking lot a small voice out of nowhere said, *"This is Holy ground."*

I parked, got out of the car and walked toward the entrance of the church. As I entered the building I began to sing a song that was bursting on the inside of me. I don't know what came over me but I had to get the song out. I was singing like I had never sang before:

Now behold the lamb the precious Lamb of God,
why you love me so I'll never know,
born into sin that I may live again
why you love me so I'll never know.
When I always didn't do right,
I went left you told me to go right.
But I'm standing right here in the mist of my tears.
Claiming you to be the Lamb of God.
The precious Lamb of God.

I was singing with my whole mind, soul and body. Tears were running down my face and I kept right on praising God.

Dwayne appeared out of nowhere. I saw him walking toward me with his arms outstretched and I walked right into them crying as he embraced me.
I got myself under control after a few minutes and pulled out of his arms. He motioned for me to sit on the pew next to him. I sat down.

Nicki I'm not that monster that you think I am. When I met you I was working on me. I was not ready for a wife or a relationship. But you were so beautiful to me and I wanted you so bad. I know that I deceived you but I knew if I told you that I wasn't who you thought I was you would not have given me a second look. I'm asking for your forgiveness now. I know that I talked you into doing things that wasn't right but I was a different guy back then. I'm really trying to make this thing right with us. I could not say anything so I just sat there and let him talk. We both did things back then that we both knew was wrong. The bible teaches us that we all have sinned and come short of the glory of God. I'm just trying now to get it right. I know that me marrying Dasha is a shock to you and I'm sorry but I need you to understand that what we had was wrong because I wasn't right. Do you understand that?

I finally found my voice. I looked at him and asked him the questions I'd just gotten the courage to ask.

Did you ever love me? Did I mean anything to you?

I tried to love you. I wanted you to be the one, but if I said the sky was green you would look up and confirm that it was green. I needed someone that was honest and real about everything. Not someone to stroke my ego. Dasha saw me for who I was. Trying to be someone I wasn't. She never let me get away with anything. She pushed me into things that I thought I wasn't ready for or thought I couldn't handle. She wanted me to reach my destiny. My God given destiny. I've asked God for forgiveness now I'm asking you.

I began to cry again.

I forgive you Dwayne and I'm asking you to forgive me also.

We stayed there side by side for a while. I was thinking how much God really must love me to give me mercy and grace right there on that front pew with Dwayne by my side.

Finally Dwayne got up to leave. He touched my cheek and let me with a word.

Your deliverance is in your praise.

Then he walked away just the way he appeared. I sat a little while longer wondering how I could just forgive the man who had ripped out my heart.

I passed Pastor Willis as I was going to my car. He had a smile on his face. I'm sure he knew that I'd just received healing.

As I sat in my car awhile longer, I thought about God's goodness and then I smiled too.

I started my car, headed home to shower and prepare for work the next day.

God's Favor

The next morning I was up early and I thought I would just go out for breakfast. I pulled in at I-hop, went in and decided to sit down for breakfast.

When I walked in, the first thing I noticed was this man sitting in the back of the restaurant. He had the most gorgeous smile I had seen on a man in a while. I smiled back and kept walking.

When the waitress came over to take my order she told me that the guy in the back had paid for my meal. I was shocked. When I looked back to thank him, he was gone. I just sat back and really enjoyed my free meal.

After I finished I wanted to give the waitress a big tip but she wouldn't take it she told me her name was Rhonda and that the guy that paid for my meal was her brother and he had taken care of the tip as well. I told her my name was Nicki Williams and to thank her brother for me. Rhonda and I talked for the next half hour like we had been friends forever.

Rhonda had been in Florida only six months. She was from Jersey but had always wanted to live somewhere sunny and thought what better place than Florida. Her strict upbringing demanded that she be in church. Since being in Florida, she'd visited Mt. Nebo on several occasions and found herself liking the people there very much. She had even told her brother about the church and he and Pastor Willis had begun having regular phone conversations. When Rhonda decided to join the church a couple of weeks ago she met with Pastor Willis.

I'm so happy to meet you and am glad that you will be attending Mt. Nebo. It's a wonderful church and the people are really caring. I know you will love it as much as I do.

I'm happy too, Rhonda said. Now I'd better get back to work before I get fired!

The two women laughed, exchanged phone numbers and Nicki headed to work. When she arrived, on her desk was a single rose with a card that read, 'You're special'.

All day long she wondered where that single rose came from. Nobody at the office seemed to know.

After work, Nicki stopped by her mom's house.

Something smells good.

As I sat down at the kitchen table, I watched my mom stirring a big pot on the stove. When she turned around she was smiling.

Grab a bowl and try my soup.

I love my mom's soup so I wasted no time in diving in.

How was your day sweetheart?

It was wonderful mom I got a single rose and nobody seems to know where it came from.

Did it come with a card?

It did and the card just said, "You are special."

You'll find out, I know you will.

I went to breakfast this morning and the waitress brother paid for my breakfast then disappeared before I could thank him, I thought that was strange.

Why? What was strange about being favored by God?

Mom I'm not talking about favor just the guy that paid for my meal.

Child stop over thinking things so much. Ain't nothing strange about God's favor! Live each day as though it is your last one and you'll be ok.

Mom do you love Pastor Willis?

He makes me so happy, I haven't been this happy since your father passed. I never imagined that I would ever remarry.

I am truly happy for you I want you to know that I love you and I thank you for all the wisdom and knowledge that you have instilled in me, I know that I haven't been all that I should have been and I've done some foolish things that I'm not proud of. I want you to know that I'm changing for the better and I thank you for being my mom.

I love you too baby.

She walked over and hugged me tight.

Now let's talk about this wedding, Monica can go this Saturday with us to fit my dress and find you girls something to match me. I don't want a big fuss about a big wedding. Ron and I decided that we would have a private ceremony with just my girls and my best friend Chiante, his brother Jim and his friend James. Then on Sunday after church we would have a big reception in the church hall so that the congregation can be part of the celebration. On Monday we fly to Vegas and return Sunday for service.

Mom that sounds amazing. And like a lot of work too!

Yes and we've got less than a month to get everything in order. Child if it was left up to me we would just slip away and be done with it.

You wouldn't dare deprive us of marrying you off.

We both laughed.

Thanks for the soup. I need to go by the store on my way home so I better get going. I love you mom.

Love you to baby, be careful.

It's Complicated

I stopped by Walmart on my way home and while I was shopping I looked up and saw the man from I-Hop with the gorgeous smile walking down the aisle towards me. I smiled at him and held out my hand to shake his.

I wanted to tell you thank you for breakfast this morning. My name is Nicki Williams.

Hi Nicki Williams, my name is Gregg Howard and you are welcome.

I saw you shopping and I had to come over and introduce myself. I also wanted to ask you out to dinner on Friday if you're not busy.

I thought about it for a second and decided against it.

I'm not busy but I can't.

Why not?

It's complicated.

Well at least give me your number so I can call you sometimes.

I thought, 'Ok Nicki you're moving too fast again. Wait on the Lord.'

Tell you what, if I see you again I'll give it to you if not thank you again for breakfast.

As I walked away I smiled and said 'Ok Lord if he's for me please let me run into him again.'

After I had put away my grocery I called Jackie.

Girl this week has been a rollercoaster. I talked to Dwayne.

No you didn't.

Yes I did but it's not what you're thinking. I went to church the other night and I was such a mess I began to sing and praise God and while I was singing he walked in. We had a heart to heart talk and we both decided to forgive each other. Then on yesterday I went to I-hop for breakfast and this guy paid for my food and tonight I ran back into him and he asked me out and I said no.

What? Wait a minute you're leaving details out. Slow down. You're telling me that a guy paid for your food and then asked you out and you turned him down.

Yes but I didn't know who he was until last night. He showed up at Walmart while I was getting grocery. I introduced myself and he told me his name was Gregg Howard.

Did he tell you where he worked or anything?

No and I didn't ask he asked for my phone number and I didn't give him that either.

Are you crazy?

No I just want to be sure this time you know my track record is not the greatest. I've been down this road before and I'm not taking any more chances on not getting it right.

I hear you girl.

So any way my mom's wedding is in a month and on Saturday we are going to pick out our dresses. She don't want a big wedding just a small ceremony at home with a few friends then on Sunday a big reception for their church family.

Wow I would have expected a huge wedding seeing how big that church is.

Not so girl and she's determined to have it her way.

Well it is her wedding. I better be invited to both.

You know you are part of the family and you'll be at both.

So how are you going to get to know this Gregg if you didn't give him your number.

I don't know but I told God if it's meant to be I will see him again.

After getting ready for bed I said my prayers this time including Gregg and went to sleep.

Announcements & Surprises

O
n my way home Monica called to confirm Saturday.

Did you hear that Pastor Willis is introducing the new assistant Pastor on Sunday?

I thought that they were still looking for one.

Girl where have your mind been lately? He's been talking about it for the last six months. And on last Sunday he announced that they had found an associate Pastor and he will be introduced to the congregation on Sunday.

I wonder who it will be.

Maybe mom knows. Have you spoken with her?

I stopped by yesterday but she was excited about the wedding.

Oh well we will just have to wait until Sunday.

I'll see you on Saturday bye girl.

Bye.

On Saturday I was up early and on my way to pick up mom she had decided that we would go to breakfast first and I wanted to go to I-hop praying that we would run into Gregg.

After parking I was out of the car so fast I forgot mom was in it.

Girl what you rushing for?

I tried to act normal and looked back at her impatiently.

I'm not rushing.

Mom just smiled and shook her head. Monica was already seated when we got inside. I was scanning the place like a spy hoping to see Gregg but he wasn't there.

The restaurant was packed and soon Rhonda came over to our table. After introducing her to my mother, she took our order and left.

She looks so familiar, mom said. *I think I've seen her somewhere before. When she comes back I'll ask her.*

Rhonda came back with our food and mom told her that she looked familiar.

Well like I told Nicki, I visited Mt. Nebo a couple of weeks ago and met with Pastor Ron. I talked to him at length about becoming a member of the church. I thought you looked familiar too. He told me that he was getting married soon.

Well how about that. Yes we are. Oh I remember now. I peeked in on him that day to tell him I was leaving and that's when I saw you. I'm sorry that we were not introduced. So now I know who you are, welcome to the city and to Mt. Nebo!

Thank you so much and I want you to know that this Sunday I plan to join.

I was so excited for Rhonda that I jumped up and hugged her.

I'm so happy that you will be a member and I pray that you join the choir. We will love to have you so please consider it.

We finished our breakfast and went shopping for Mom's wedding. We found everything we needed. Jackie surprised us at the dress shop and even paid for my mom's dress.

Give Him Some Praise

S unday morning the sun was shining brightly as I stepped out my front door for church. I parked in my usual spot at church. I was in such a rush to get to the choir room that I ran right into Dasha almost knocking her down.

I'm so sorry Dasha I wasn't looking where I was going are you alright?

Yes I'm ok it's alright. Now that we are face to face I wanted to talk to you for a minute. Look I know that you hate me right now but I wanted to apologize for what has happened. I'm asking your forgiveness. I can't say that it was all Dwayne fault nor mines but he told me that you and he was finished. After we got together he told the truth. Will you forgive me?

I've been meaning to call you anyway and talk to you about this situation. I'm glad I bumped into you also. I have to forgive you maybe you are the best thing for him I don't know all I know is that he and I talked and I wasn't good for him. Its ok Dasha I'm not angry anymore God has delivered me from that. Now let's go and give him some praise!

Church was awesome! I felt great! While I was singing my song, Pastor Ron and the new associate walked into the church and I almost forgot the words to the song I was singing. The new associate Pastor was Gregg Howard! I almost went down on my knees, my voice started to shake and Jackie noticed that I was looking kind of crazy and took over the song. I never been so thankful in all my life!

After the choir sang Pastor Ron stepped up to the podium and started to speak.

It is a pleasure for me to introduce to you all a fine and upcoming man of God. Pastor Gregg Howard comes to us from our sister church in Jersey and he's going to be our new associate pastor, a power house for God. Please stand and give him a Mt. Nebo welcome!

Everybody stood and clapped so hard you would have thought Pastor Ron had introduced God. The clapping finally stopped and Gregg stepped up to the podium. Silence fell over the congregation. I could see the single women in our church already claiming him as their husband in their heads. When he began to speak every eye was on him.

Good afternoon Mt. Nebo. As Pastor said, my name is Pastor Gregg Howard and it is my honor and pleasure to begin my new journey here at Mt. Nebo. As Pastor Ron said, I come from Jersey. My sister Rhonda and I thought this would be the perfect place to call home. Rhonda would you stand please.

Rhonda stood up and everybody clapped for her.

Would you like to say a few words Rhonda?

Yes, Pastor Howard, thank-you. Again, I'm Rhonda Howard and I would like to say thank you all for welcoming me to your church. I feel right at home. I hope to become a valuable member of this great congregation. My brother and I believe in praising and worshipping God. Thank you all again for making us feel right at home.

As Rhonda sat down, Pastor Gregg finished his speech.

I believe in the power of God and I know that everything works together for the good of those who love the Lord. I love the Lord so I know that working with all of you will be good.

As he sat back down Pastor Ron got up.

As you all know in less than four months I'll be on my honeymoon and during that time you will be under the leadership of Pastor Howard. I expect you all to treat him with the dignity and respect that you give me. Pastor Howard will be heading up our single's ministry and Sister Rhonda will be assisting him.

Meant To Be

After service both Pastors and Rhonda were invited to mom's house for dinner. Jackie met me in the parking lot.

Girl is that the Gregg you were talking about?

Yes that's him and you know the funny thing about it is I told him that if we were meant to be together we'll see each other again...never in a million years I would have thought that he was a pastor.

Girl I'm not missing this dinner for nothing! I'm following you there.

On the way to mom's house I thought about what I would say to him now that I knew he was a pastor. My mind was so occupied that I almost ran a light. When I arrived at mom's the driveway was full and the street in front of the house also, so I parked two houses up with Jackie right on my tail. She practically ran me down.

What are you going to do now?

I don't know I guess I'm going to act naturally like this sort of thing happens all the time.

You know you're not that good of an actress.

I know but everybody is in there so maybe it won't be that bad.

Mom opened the door and ushered us inside. Once inside the house was in full swing with everybody trying to do everything at once to prepare the tables for dinner, Jackie and I just stepped right in to help. I was dishing up bowls of food and passing them to the next person to put on the tables. Gregg came up beside me and whispered in my ear.

Now can I have your number?

I almost dropped the bowl I was holding.

Yes, I said. Silently praying that he not stand so close to me.

When the tables were ready, mom asked everyone for silence as Pastor Gregg offered the blessings. When he'd finished, the house became lively again with everybody trying to talk at once.

After dinner, Jackie and I were in the kitchen washing up dishes and talking about Gregg.

Did he ask you for your number again?

Yes, but I haven't had the chance to give it to him yet.

While we were talking, Gregg walked in and asked for a glass of water.

Jackie excused herself on the pretense of going to make sure no dishes were left in the dining room. I busied myself with getting him some water.

I wanted to tell you that you sing beautiful and you are very talented.

Thank you. Why didn't you tell me that you were a pastor?

I didn't think that it was important. Would it have made a difference?

No, I don't think it would have. Here's my number.

I'll give you a call tonight and we can talk more tonight.

As soon as he walked out Jackie rushed back in.

What he say?

Nothing much I gave him my number and he's going to call me tonight.

If you don't call me afterwards I'll kill you I'm dying to know what he has to say.

You know I'll call you.

I went to tell my mom and Pastor Willis goodnight and Jackie and I walked out together.

Friends, Family & Wisdom

L ater that evening I was so wired up waiting for Gregg to call. I kept looking at my cell wondering what time he would call and not wanting to miss him.

At nine my phone rang and the caller ID said Gregg Howard!

Hello?

Nicki how are you?

Good and you?

I'm more than good. Now is there anything you would like to know about me? I can tell you that I'm thirty-two my birthday is July eighth and I have never been married nor do I have children. I would love to have a house full one day. I work first of all for God and I'm a CEO for Georgia Power. I saw you walk in at i-hop and you captured my heart I knew that I had to get to know you. When a man is sure of whom he is and to whom he belongs he knows what he wants and Nicki I want to get to know you better. Now tell me something about you that you think I should know.

I'm finding my way. I've been through a lot mostly because of my doing. I work as a social worker for the city of Jacksonville and most days I'm home by five then on other days it's whenever. I have one sister, one niece, and a brother-in-law that I love dearly. The girl that was with me tonight was my best friend Jackie. I want to get to know you better also.

This is a start don't you think?

I have a speaking engagement coming up soon. Would you like to come with me? The conference should be interesting and between the sessions maybe we can have dinner, see the sights and get to know each other.

Sure, I'd love that.

Great. I'll be in touch later with the details.

We talked a bit longer and then hung up with the promise to stay in touch.

I called Jackie and when she answered I told her that Gregg was the guy I was going to marry.

You couldn't possibly know that girl stop talking silly and tell me what he said.

He said that he knows I'm the woman for him. He also asked me to ride with him to church. That's a good thing right?

You know it is. Keep me posted.
You know I will!

After we hung up I got on my knees and thanked God for friends, family and wisdom:

Father, I am so amazed by the way you love me. To think that you are jealous for me, simply rocks my world. I know me and cannot comprehend why you love me so much, but God by sheer faith I thank you and praise you for loving me and pursuing me even when I didn't want to be found. Thank you for never letting me go. Help me to love you more and share that love with friends and family. In Jesus' sweet name I pray. Amen.

Blacked Out

M om's wedding was beautiful. She was the most beautiful bride I had ever seen. Monica and I cried through the whole ceremony. The reception was packed. Gregg looked so handsome in his suit and I was so proud of him. We had grown closer in the past four months and were now officially a couple.

During the reception, Mom came over to where Monica and I were standing and gave us a big kiss and whispered in our ears.

Thank you girls for everything you two did to make this day special for us. Ron and I thank you from the bottom of our hearts.

We hugged her hard and wished her a safe trip.

Monica looked at me and said that she and Ryan had a busy day and they both were tired and going home for some much needed rest.

Gregg came over, kissed me and asked if I needed a ride home. I told him no I was going to help Jackie and the other church members clean up and I would call him later.

On the way home I was thinking how far God had brought me and all that he had done for me and didn't see the car in front of me had stalled in the middle of the street. Before I could react I plowed into the back of it causing the car behind me to hit me. The impact was so hard that I blacked out.

Pastor Gregg's Prayer

P astor Ron, this is Pastor Gregg. I hate to call you and Mother Christine at this late hour but Nicki has been in an accident and is in surgery now at Mount Sini hospital.

What happened?

I'm not exactly sure but she hit a stalled car and the car behind her was speeding and couldn't stop before hitting her. All they would tell us is that she suffered head injuries, and some broken bones.

Her mom and I will catch the next flight out.

I'm so sorry Pastor. Please tell Mother Christine. I should have been with Nicki – protecting her.

Son, this is not your fault. Are you there alone?

No, I'm here with Monica, Ryan, Jackie and some other church members.

Good. You all pray and lean on each other. Christine and I will be there as soon as we can.

Thank you Pastor Ron. We will be here waiting for you. I'll send someone to pick you two up at the airport.

Keep the faith son. I'll call you back with our flight information.

I hung the phone up and began to pray to God like never before.

God I know you didn't let me find her just to take her. I should have stayed and followed her home. What was I thinking? She had to pull through this.

I had proposed to Nicki on Saturday. I knew from the beginning that she would be my wife.

God please hear my prayer!

My cell rang back. It was Mother Christine on the other end.

Gregg, Pastor told me what you said. Son, don't you go blaming yourself for this. I don't know what God is doing but we have to trust him and believe that he's going to work this out.

Ok Mother Christine. Thank you.

Our flight will be in at twelve. In the meantime, I expect you to be strong for Nicki. You know the words of prayer and you know that prayer is powerful so let's pray.

After Nicki's mom and I prayed, calmness came over me like I've never known as if I knew she was going to make it through this. I began to thank God for his healing:

Father God I love you and am so thankful for the hope that life holds because I know you! I praise you and I thank you that Nicki is not alone nor will she ever be. She lacks nothing because you are her provider. Your grace is always sufficient. Thank you for healing. Your words tell us that by your strips we are healed. Lord keep Nicki as the apple of your eye. Hide her under the shadow of your wings and we will be so faithful in giving you all the praise and honor. In the Mighty Name of Jesus, It Is So Done! Amen.

Jackie's Proposal

Jackie had more time on her hands than she knew what to do with. All her life she had been labeled the good girl. Not that she thought that she just never wanted to disappoint her grandmother who had raised her since she was two.

Her mom had been in the military and was stationed in Italy and could not take Jackie with her.

On Jackie's tenth birthday she learned that her mother had been killed by a stray bullet and had it not been for her grandmother, Jackie knew she would surly have lost her mind.

GG, as she affectionately called her beloved grandmother, was the best thing in her life.

Jackie had not dated a lot because GG always said that she was set aside for God's best. Jackie knew her worth and always was careful of how she carried herself.

About a year ago she met and fell in love with Sherman, Mother Christine's best friend Chiante's son. They had decided to keep it quiet until they knew where the relationship was going.

The hardest thing had been not telling Nicki about it. Now Nicki was laid up in ICU not knowing if she was even in this world.

Jackie was sitting in the waiting room full of family and friends praying for her best friend's healing.

Sherman walked in, went over to his mother, gave her a hug and kiss on the cheek and said something to her. He looked around the room until he spotted me. I couldn't take my eyes off him as he walked toward me.

Oh yeah he was fine, tall and chocolate. I remembered the first time he spoke to me. My tongue was almost caught in my throat. But thank God I found my voice.

He sat next to me and just touched my arm while I cried like a baby.

Let's just walk outside for a few seconds so that you can get some fresh air.

On the walk down he assured me that everything was going to be alright.
Baby, where is your faith?

It's not my faith Sherman it's just that she looks so bad laying in there all broken up and everything.

Has anyone talked to her mom yet?

Yes, Pastor Gregg called them. They will be in around twelve. We hated to call them but we had no other choice.

I know that Nicki was daydreaming again. She always does that. I've told her time and time again that she has to keep her mind on what she's doing at all times.

Baby, what happened?

She stayed late to help clean up and on her way home a car had stalled in the street and she hit it and the car behind her hit her. She was so excited about her proposal that I know she was daydreaming.

What are the doctors saying?

Monica and her husband are the only ones the doctors have spoken with and they are waiting until Pastor Ron and Mother Christine get here to share the news. I guess all we can do now is wait.

Baby don't you know the doctors on staff tonight?

Yea and they are doing everything that they can.

So, don't worry. Things have a way of working themselves out.

I know it's just hard to see her like this. Why didn't she ride with Gregg?

You know Nicki she has a mind of her own. I'm pretty sure he's wondering the same thing. Did you speak with him?

Yea I talked with him for a while. He's strong and he's praying. He told me that God didn't bring him this far to leave him.

That sounds so much like something he would say.

How is your mom holding up I talked to her when she first arrived.

Mom's a prayer warrior she won't leave until Nicki's mom gets here. Who's picking them up at the airport?

Everybody is preoccupied so maybe we should go get them.

Let me grab my purse tell everyone we are going and I'll be right back.

On the drive there we talked about everything except the accident. The plane landed on time and we met Nicki's parents at the baggage claim area. Pastor and Mrs. Willis were so glad to see us. She hugged me so tight all the while whispering in my ear that everything will be all right.

On the way back to the hospital I filled them in on everything I knew. Sherman let them out at the front of the hospital and then we went continued on to the parking deck.

He turned to me and pulled me into his arms and kissed me.

I've been waiting all night to do that. I've been thinking what if that were you in there? I couldn't bear to live without you. I've wanted to ask you to be my wife for a long time now and I think that now is the right time. Jackie Denise Jones will you do me the honor of becoming my wife? I promise that you will never regret it.

Sherman took a small box out of his glove compartment, opened it and slipped a ring on my finger.

I'm so sure now that this is the right time. Baby will you marry me?

With tears in my eyes I could only nod my head yes.

You have made me the happiest man on earth.

He took me in his arms and planted kisses all over my face.

But what will I say if someone notices my ring?

Say he asked and I said yes and we'll go from there.

I thought about it and it just didn't seem right to do this without Nicki.

I want to wait until I can tell my best friend. Is that ok with you baby?

Ok I'll let you do it your way for now.

I took the ring off and put it on my necklace until Nicki could celebrate my happiness with me.

GG's Story

Around three in the morning most of the people that had come out started to go home. Pastor Ron asked the remaining to gather around for a word of prayer. After he prayed we sat back down and waited for the doctor to come in.

An hour passed before the doctor came in. He looked tired. Are the parents here yet? Pastor and Mother Christine stood up and approached the doctor. After they stepped in the hallway I looked at Sherman and he squeezed my hand.

After a time, Mother Christine came back in looking relieved.

Nicki has a long journey ahead but she will be ok. There is swelling to her head, she has a broken arm, and her hip was broken but with prayer and the right therapist she will walk again.

Everybody breathed a sigh of relief.

Pastor and I want you to go home and get some rest. Thank you for being here and for your prayers.

Outside of the hospital, Sherman continued to show concern.

I know you don't think that I'm letting you drive home do you?

I'm ok just a little tired but I know I can make it home.

No baby I'm not taking any chances.

I'll take you home and bring you back tomorrow to get your car after you have gotten some rest.

I agreed and allowed him to drive me home. The second I walked in the house, GG called to see how everything was.

Who told you and what are you doing still up?

Girl I may be old but not much get past me.

GG was eighty seven years old and acted like she was fifty. Everybody treated her like she belonged to them.

Around my twenty-seventh birthday, GG sat me down and told me her story.

I never knew my mother or my father. I was raised by an older cousin and her husband. I never knew when I stopped being a child and became a woman. All I remember is that I thought it was natural for a grown man to take a child to bed and sleep with them. My cousin knew what was happening to me but she was afraid of her husband because he beat her. So the things that went on in our house seemed natural to me. It wasn't until I was in grade school and saw that the other girls looked and acted different that I began to realize that I was different. I met Molly Gilbert and she became my best friend. The first time I was allowed to stay overnight in her home I was shocked that her father didn't come in her bedroom that night! In the morning at the breakfast table we was told to bow our heads for this thing called prayer, something that was never done in my home. After prayer they shared their thoughts with joy and everybody was allowed to talk. When it was my turn, I asked Molly's father why he didn't come into Molly's room to sleep with her at night. The table got quite and everybody looked at me like I had lost my mind. Molly's mom and dad took me in another part of the house, sat me down, asked me if that happened at my house and I told them my story because I didn't know that it was a shameful and disgusting thing that my cousin's husband was doing to me. From that day forward the Gilbert's became my family. I never knew what happened to my cousin until I was in college. The Gilbert's had gotten a court order and a conviction for both my cousin and her husband. They saved me and I didn't know what I was being saved from. Oh I know that my cousin was afraid of her husband but I was a child. She was suppose to protect me from all hurt and harm. Over the next decade I tried to gather information about her, but to no avail. The Gilbert's taught me how to pray and how to become the woman that I became. I worked hard in college, became a teacher and an advocate for child abuse. That's why I'm so hard on you.

With tears in my eyes, I made a vow that GG would never be ashamed or disappointed in me. I know that GG's life couldn't have been easy all those years ago but I thanked God that she made a difference in mine. I have followed her advice and guidance all my life and she never gave me bad advice.

How Could That Be?

Back at the hospital Pastor Ron and Christine were going through something that the doctor told them in private. It had totally blown them away. Nicki was not the only one laying in that hospital bed fighting for her life - she was carrying a child!

Christine looked at her husband and asked a question she knew he could not answer.

How could that be?

Ron could not think of a reasonable answer.

I think that Gregg and I need to sit down and have a long talk.

Not without me! Who do they think they are? Did they think that God wouldn't reveal this thing to us?

Now calm down Christine. Getting upset will do no one any good. Doctor Henry said he only told us because if things get scary he would have to abort the pregnancy.

But Christine seemed inconsolable.

How could they do this? This is bad, so bad. I don't know what to do. She's in a coma fighting for her life and I wonder if she even knows that she's pregnant? My God Ron I can't believe she and Gregg did not know this!

Don't let this worry you honey. I'm going to call Gregg now.

Oh Lord

G regg could not seem to sleep. As he looked out the window of his house he thought about meeting and falling in love with Nicki; how she smiled, how she smelled and every good thing about her.

Gregg's mind went back to one night four months ago when he and Nicki went to Atlanta for a preaching engagement that he couldn't get out of. He had already made reservations for a hotel room before he met Nicki and after they started seeing each other he invited her along.

Nicki accepted and that week-end had been so special. They arrived at the Peachtree Plaza Hotel in downtown Atlanta mid- morning. Gregg assumed that another room would be available, but unfortunately all the rooms were booked because TD Jakes was in town.

They searched all over Atlanta for any available rooms but all was taken. By mid-afternoon they gave up, had lunch and went back to his room for a quick nap.

Once inside the room they both were quiet and Gregg looked at Nicki.

We can handle this can't we?

Yes. Sure we can. Nicki assured him. *We are both adults and you are a man of God so I have nothing to worry about.*

Nicki you know that I love you, but I am still human. Let's try to get some sleep. I'll take the couch and you can take the bedroom and please lock the door just in case I sleepwalk!

Ha-Ha very funny. Nicki laughed nervously.

Look Nicki we are getting married and I don't want you to be uncomfortable with me being so close to you in this room so I'll go sleep in the car.

Don't you dare! Nicki said. *We can handle this. I know we can.*

Nicki walked into the bathroom and shut the door. A few seconds later I heard the shower come on. My mind just went crazy thinking about how she smelled, how she looked and what she was doing with the soap and the wash towel. I had to get out of the room quick, fast and in a hurry.

I went outside and walked the grounds of the hotel talking to God. After my nerves calmed down I began to pray to God for strength to get through tonight and tomorrow night with Nicki sharing my room.

I thought about finding a pastor in the hotel and just marrying her right then, I don't know what came over me. I had never felt this way about a woman in my life.

A song came in my spirit and I began to sing.

Oh Lord I want you to help me,
help me,
singing oh Lord I need you to help me,
help me on my journey
help me on my way
oh Lord I need you to help me!
God I'm your child help me!

Afterwards I felt so much better. When I got back to the room Nicki was asleep. As I looked at her my heart swelled up with so much love that I almost passed out. At that moment I knew I loved her so much and that I had found the woman that I wanted to spend the rest of my life with.

I went into the bathroom, took a cold shower and laid down on the couch for a couple of hours. I felt something brush my face. When I felt it again and opened my eyes I saw Nicki standing over me smiling. I smiled back and pulled her down on the couch and began tickling her as I did. She hit at me playfully and we both rolled on the floor.

You can wake me up like this anytime, I love you so much and I can hardly wait to make you my wife.

It won't be long Gregg. Only a few more months and I'll be Mrs. Gregg Howard.

Come on we better get dressed. Church starts at seven.

Promises & Deceptions

The event went well and afterwards we found a little café on a side street off of Piedmont Road. It was not crowded and the service was great. After we ate, we decided to walk back to the hotel. During our walk Gregg told Nicki over again how beautiful she looked in her yellow sundress.

I don't think I tell you enough Nicki how beautiful you are. I want you to know that I'll never hurt you and that I'll do my best to make you happy for the rest of our life. If you are ever unhappy about anything talk to me, don't ever hold anything back from me, that's all I ask of you. My mom and dad were married a long time and although they disagreed on some things they kept the communication opened. They never went to bed angry. Promise me you'll always talk to me no matter what.

I promise. Nicki agreed.

Gregg leaned in and gave her the sweetest kiss. When they opened their eyes, it was hard to tell which of them had the biggest smile.

I love you so much and I promise you that I'll never do anything to make you frown. I love your smile it's like a ray of sunshine on a cold day.

You put that smile on my face you do know that don't you? I want to see you smile for the rest of my life I want our son or daughter your smile. We never talked about children, how many you want or if you even want any.

Gregg I want children. Growing up it was just Monica and me. I always wished that my mom had had another child so that mom wouldn't compare me to Monica all the time. Don't get me wrong, I love her dearly but she just thought that I should have been like Monica. I rebelled a lot back then. Monica got straight A's, I got B's, she had wavy hair, I had straight hair, she applied to college on time, I waited, she met Ryan in church, I had to be forced to go to church. I think I did those things because I didn't want to be like Monica. I gave my mom the blues for a long time if I had had another sister or brother around my age maybe I wouldn't have been so rebellious. How many children do you want?

There was always just me and Rhonda and we were as thick as thieves. I never thought about having another sibling. I protected her and she watched out for me. I would love to have at least three children maybe more. I love children and can't wait until you have our first child.

Nicki had looked at Gregg curiously then.

What is it honey?

I looked over at Gregg to see if he was serious or just joking. He was serious. I knew then I had the opening to tell him about the abortion that I had had a few years ago with Dwayne's child but I didn't want to spoil the moment. I didn't want to be deceptive but I just didn't want to open that can of worms.

As we got nearer to the hotel Gregg pulled me to him and kissed me once again.

Take My Breath Away

O nce inside the room Nicki took a shower and prepared for bed.

It's still early. Do you want to watch a movie? I had the bellboy bring up popcorn and some cokes.

Sure why not, Nicki replied sitting down next to Gregg on the couch.

You choose the movie. I said and watched her look through the collection that was there.

Oh look, one of my all-time favorites, The Notebook with James Garner and Gena Rowlands.

Gregg loved seeing Nicki happy.

While the movie was playing and we were eating popcorn Gregg kept looking at Nicki watching her reactions to the movie. Nicki was a very passionate, caring, and sensitive woman. He liked that. Before he knew what he was doing he grabbed Nicki and started kissing her with all the pent up passion that was in him.

Nicki was startled at first but then she began to kiss him with as much passion as he had. Gregg picked her up and carried her to the bedroom. Lying her down gently on the bed he undressed her and then himself.

God you're beautiful.

Then he started kissing her all over her body.

I've never felt this loved before. It's so wonderful. Nicki said.

Gregg looked Nicki into her eyes then.

Do you want me to stop?

Nicki shook her head no.

 Gregg trailed small kisses up and down her body until she screamed out his name.

Afterwards she lay in his arms and he wrapped his body around her as if to protect her and she dosed off to sleep.

Morning came too fast and again Gregg awoke to Nicki touching his face. As his eyes focused on her, she planted a kiss on his lips. Gregg pulled her down on the couch with him.

I love you so much Nicki. We really need to talk about last night. I was so out of line. I'm sorry for taking advantage of you but you make me lose sight of everything. I wanted to make love to you and I wanted you to want it too. Now that it happened I've got to make it right. All night long I sat here and thought about how to make this right in God's eyesight and in yours and mine. There are a lot of pastors here in this hotel and I know one of them will marry us. Nicki will you marry me today? Please say yes and make me the happiest man alive.

She'd quickly said yes. They kissed and held each other tight and Gregg thought he'd died and gone to heaven.

Nicki Williams, you take my breath away!

Say Something

While Gregg got dressed Nicki took her shower. By the time she was done, Gregg was already gone so she continued to get dressed and then wait for him to return.

An hour later he returned with two pastors, Pastor Walker and Pastor Smith, both had agreed to marry them and witness the union.

Gregg saw the look on Nicki's face.

What is it honey?

I'm feeling kind of bad because my family will not be able to witness the best day of my life.

It's all going to be alright. Gregg looked into her eyes and whispered in her ear.

Nicki smiled, letting him know she believed him.

I'm ready now.

The ceremony was quick and simple and after it was over Gregg and Nicki stayed in the room for the rest of the morning.

I promise you Nicki that I will make this day up to you. I know that you wanted your wedding day to be with friends and family and I promise you that it will happen. Things just got so intense last night and although it was wrong it was right in so many ways. I love you so much and I would never do anything to hurt you in any way but I knew that if I didn't marry you we both would be on our way to hell. I couldn't risk that.

I know and now I'm Mrs. Gregg Howard and it feels wonderful. I want to shout it from the rooftop and I want to call Jackie, Monica, and my mom! I just want everyone to know how happy you've made me. Are you happy Gregg?

I see your face and I'm happy Nicki. I want to spend the rest of my life making you happy. I think we need to let your mom and sister know that we got married as soon as we get home tomorrow.

On the ride home the newlyweds talked about their future and where they wanted to be in five years. Gregg wanted to have his own church and Nicki wanted that for him also.

They stopped off at a small diner for dinner. Gregg excused himself and went to the men's room to freshen up after they were seated. While he was gone, Nicki's inner voice kept reminding her that secrets would not strengthen her marriage. She knew she needed to tell Gregg about her abortion.

She didn't want to ruin this day with talking about her past but that voice in her head was persistent and insisted that she tell him NOW!

Nicki watched Gregg walk back to the table all smiles and wondered how he would react to the bomb that she was about to lay on him.

She knew that she would have to tell him eventually and made up her mind that she might as well tell him now. She wished that she had taken the opportunity to tell him the other night BEFORE they had gotten married.

Gregg sat down and asked if she'd ordered. Nicked told him that she'd been waiting for him to return.

The waitress came, took their order and left. Gregg noticed that she was a little too quiet and asked her what was bothering her.

Are you upset because of what we did? Or how we were married? Please talk to me. Tell me what's wrong.

Nicki knew that NOW was the time to tell Gregg everything about her and Dwayne.

After she finished, their dinner sat cold and untouched which described them perfectly at the moment. Gregg sat their cold like a statue, staring at Nicki but not saying anything or touching her.

Gregg please say something. Don't just sit there.

Gregg pushed his chair back, signaled for the waitress paid the bill. He waited for me to get up and we walked out of the restaurant to his car not saying a word.

He opened my car door, stepped around to the driver's side and we pulled onto the highway headed back home. An hour went by without Gregg saying a word. Nicki couldn't take it another second so she spoke to him.

Where Do We Go From Here?

Where do we go from here? Can you talk to me I need to hear to say something. I know I should have told you this before we got married. I just couldn't find the right time and then everything just started to happen so fast. I got caught up in the moment and I didn't want to spoil anything that was happening. Gregg say something. Anything.

It was another twenty minutes before Gregg spoke and when he did, Nicki thought her heart would break in two.

Nicki what you did was deceptive and all I can say right now is I don't know if I can stay married to you. I have to talk to God and pray that this marriage can survive this. When we get home I'm going to drop you off and go home. When I make up my mind about us I'll give you an answer.

Gregg dropped Nicki off at home and drove off. Her steps were heavy as well as her heart as she entered her home. She wanted to call somebody, anybody to talk to but she couldn't because nobody even knew she was married.

Nicki lay in bed thinking about what had just happened and cried for not trusting herself enough to tell the man that she loved about her past.

All night long she tossed and turned until finally she got up, got her my bible and went to the scriptures for an answer. She found herself at **2 Chronicles 7:14** and there she found the comfort she had been seeking.

Nicki knew that she had turned from her wicked ways, humbled herself and that God had forgiven her for what she'd done so long ago. She just wanted to know why Gregg was not as forgiving as God had been.

She cried for the mistrust she had placed in his heart over her. She cried for the unforgiving heart of Gregg's, and then she began to pray for both of them, for their marriage and that it wouldn't be over.

Nicki tried calling Gregg but he wouldn't answer his cell or his house phone.

G regg stood still as he stared out into the night. He was praying and asking God first for forgiveness and then for direction. He refused to let his mind wonder or think about anything other than what God wanted him to do next.

This decision would affect the rest of his life. When he talked to God, he always stood looking out at the universe and waited for an answer. Sometimes the answer came quick and other times he had to wait a while but the answer always came.

An hour later God spoke to Gregg's spirit and gave him a scripture to read. He stepped away from the window, sat at his desk and took out his bible and searched for the scripture that God had laid on his heart.

In **Proverbs 18:22** Gregg read, "A man who finds a wife finds a good thing and obtains favor from the Lord." He pondered this for a long time. He knew that his decision wouldn't come tonight. As he got ready for bed his phone rang. As he looked down, he saw that it was Nicki calling him and he chose not to answer her call.

What God Has To Say

The next morning Gregg was meditating when his phone rang so he ignored it. Two hours later he decided to shower, get dressed and go talk to Nicki.

The doorbell rang causing Nicki to almost jump out of her skin. She looked out and saw her husband standing there looking more handsome than she had ever seen him and she cried out in joy.

Nicki opened the door and let Gregg in. Once inside she led him to the den and offered him coffee. Gregg declined the coffee, took her hand and they both sat down on the couch.

I need to talk and I need you to listen to what I have to say.

Nicki nodded her head and Gregg continued.

Why you waited to tell me I don't understand but you did and now I'm waiting to hear what God has to say. So while we wait, I've decided that we tell no one about the marriage. We will still go on as if we are still dating and I will help you with everything or anything that you need help with. I found a good thing in you Nicki and I'm just hurt right now. We won't live together as man and wife until I'm certain that there is and will be no more secrets between us. I love you with all my heart and I don't know why you thought you had to keep secrets. I'm not even sure we'll ever have kids, are you? I want kids - lots of kids, but you've gone and done this. What if you can't conceive because of what you did? Did you think of that? I wanted little girls with that beautiful smile of yours. I wanted to feel them inside you. I wanted so much to see you carrying my children. I can't think right now so give me time. I'll call you when I'm ready to talk again.

Gregg kissed Nicki when they got to the door and she wanted more but he walked out of the house without looking back leaving her to stare at his back as he got in the car and pulled off.

 A week passed without her hearing from him. She'd seen him at church and mid-week service but they'd only spoke to one another in passing.

She wanted to tell Jackie what had happened but she seemed preoccupied with something in her own life. Nicki wanted to tell her mom but all mom could talk about was the wedding and Pastor Ron.

Nicki waited for Gregg's call every day for a week. Finally the doorbell rang late one night and her heart jumped in her chest - it had to be Gregg. Who else would come over this late at night?

Nicki peeped out and saw that it was Jackie, Monica, and her mom. What a surprise it was. She opened the door and they came marching in like a small army with her niece in tow.

To what do I owe this honor?

Monica gave me Alesia as they all got comfortable on my couch and oversized chair.

We are trying to go over last minute details before the wedding. We've all been so busy that we couldn't seem to get together, so we decided to invade your home.

Before I could answer the doorbell rang again. I went to answer it and saw Rhonda and Chiante standing there with enough food to feed an army. I let them in and went to the kitchen to get drinks for everyone.

Soon everyone was eating and talking and putting the last touches on the wedding. I looked over at my niece who was asleep in Rhonda's arms.

Let me lay her down and then we can get back to the wedding, I told Rhonda.

After kissing her chubby cheeks I lay her down on my bed and went back to join the others.

Three hours later we were in agreement that there was nothing else left to discuss. Someone looked at the clock and it was pass eleven so everyone started to leave, but Jackie said that she was staying the night so that she and I could catch up.

Monica started to my bedroom to get the baby and I told her to leave her go spend some alone time with Ryan and I would drop her off after breakfast. She left so fast that Jackie and I laughed long after her car had pulled out of my driveway.

Sherman and I have been dating for a year. He asked me to marry him. Jackie blurted out.

I was shocked. My mouth dropped open and it was a few seconds before I found my voice.

What? You and Sherman have been dating for a year and you didn't even tell me your best friend? How could you keep that from me? When, how, when do you guys go out? It's like I don't even know you, I thought we were best friends for life.

Jackie looked sad for a second then we both sat down on the couch and she told me the story.

They met then started to date, fell in love and decided to wait before having sex. He was celibate also.

I wanted to tell you so many times but I knew you would judge me.

What me Judge you? Girl please I'm the last person to judge after all I've done in my lifetime. You were there you know I was no saint. Now I deal with my past and leave it where it belongs in my past.

I wanted to tell Jackie about my wedding my breakup and everything that had happened with Gregg and I but I didn't know so I couldn't tell her I kept quiet. I reached over and hugged her.

I'm so happy for you. I'm so proud of you. Have you decided on a date yet?

I didn't accept his proposal yet. I haven't given him an answer because he didn't give a ring. I thought he was teasing.

Girl he was probably just testing you to see if you were feeling him the way he's feeling you. I know he had a ring somewhere he was raised better than that.

The baby started to cry before I could tell her about Gregg and I so I went to dry her and she went to make her a bottle.

Thirty minutes later Alesia was asleep and we were back on the couch sharing popcorn and watching a movie. I was the first to dose off. I had my phone on vibrate so I didn't hear it ring. Jackie answered it.

Hello. Is this Nicki?

Hi Gregg. No, this is Jackie. Nicki is asleep.

Oh Ok. How are you Jackie?

I'm fine Gregg and you?

I'm good also. Well, please tell Nicki that I called.

I sure will.

Jackie put a blanket over Nicki and tip toed to the guest room.

Love Jones

The sun woke Nicki the next morning. She looked at my cell for the time and realized it was already ten thirty and she had not heard the baby wake up.

She got up to go check on her and maybe get a cup of coffee. She heard the baby laugh and Jackie talking to her. Nicki found the two of them in the guest bathroom. Alesia was covered in bubbles and to her delight, Aunt Jackie was blowing them at her and she was giggling and trying to catch them.

Well what do we have here?

You were sleeping so peaceful when she woke up so I got her. We didn't want to wake you so I ran her a bubble bath. Oh by the way Gregg called last night I told him you were tired and I didn't want to wake you.

I looked at her as if she had lost her mind.

You did what? Why didn't you wake me? Did he say what he wanted? How long did you two talk?

Hold on. You're firing question at me so fast I don't know which one to answer first. He called late but I was still up watching the end of the movie. You know how I hate not knowing how a movie ends. Anyway, I told him you had fallen asleep and that you were tired. We talked a few minutes longer and he said to tell you he called and would see you sometime today. Are you two ok? He sounded funny on the phone last night and you're standing here looking like he was your last life line.

Everything is ok did he say when he would call back?

No just that he would see you sometime today.

Let me fix breakfast and get my shower then we can carry Alesia home so that I can make sure I'm here when he comes.

Jackie gave me a strange look but agreed to start getting dressed.

Nicki rushed through breakfast and Jackie left with the promise to meet her at the church on Friday to decorate for the wedding.

Monica could barely open the door for them before Nicki had given her the baby, waved goodbye all the while promising she would be at the church on Friday by five.

Once home she looked at the caller ID to see if Gregg had called the house phone while she was out. He hadn't and she was disappointed.

When the phone rang, she snatched it up before it could ring a second time.

Dang girl you didn't even give me a chance to thank you for watching the baby last night. What is the matter with you? You rushed out like you were going to put out a fire. Was she fussy last night?

No Monica she was the perfect angel. She woke once for a diaper change and a bottle. She ate a big breakfast and besides I promised I would have her home after breakfast.

Then what was the big rush for?

Oh you know me I wanted to get back home to wash and clean the house up so my evening would be free for Gregg.

Monica started laughing.

Girl you've got it bad. You have been bitten by love jones.

Yea I guess I have. Look I'm in the middle of sorting out my wash I'll call you later.

The Charade

After they hung up, Nicki looked at cell and house phone one last time and then decided to wash her clothes after all.

She finished all her chores and still had not heard from Gregg. The clock read three thirty so she went to the kitchen to fix a sandwich and chips. She was starving so she fixed two sandwiches and ate both of them. Even after eating them both she realized she not full so she found the bag of Oreo's she'd put in the back of the cabinet and started eating them.

When my nerves are bad, I eat!

It was after five and she was dozing when she heard a car pull up in the drive. She looked out and saw Gregg getting out of his car. Her heart did a flip flop in her chest and she sent up a prayer asking God to let them be alright.

Nicki opened the door before Gregg could ring the doorbell.

Hi come on in.

Gregg stepped in the door and before Nicki knew what was happening he was planting kisses all over her face.

Nicki I love you and I miss you.

She began to cry but not tears of sadness but joy. She was certain that he was about to either come live here or she was going to go live with him and their life together would finally begin.

Gregg sat her down on his lap, looked in her eyes and told her that they would have to wait a little while longer.

Nicki got so angry with him that she jumped up off his lap.

Why? If you are such a man of God why haven't He talked to you? What is He waiting on? You did something wrong too. You sinned too. So why am I the only one who's being punished?

Gregg felt like he'd been slapped in the face. He knew in his heart that she was right.

I am being punished. I'm not living with you as your husband am I? I haven't stood in that pulpit since we made love have I? My heart is torn in to pieces Nicki. I can't eat. I can't sleep. I'm barely functioning. I feel you next to me and when I reach out you're not there. I dream of you and when I awake - you're not there beside me. Yes

Nicki I'm being punished! I need you by my side so I propose to you that we start dating again.

Dating again? How do we go from making love to being married to dating Gregg?

We have to try Nicki if we are going to get through this.

Next Saturday mom and Pastor Ron will be married. How do I pretend that we aren't? How can I walk into that church next to you as your girlfriend?

Nicki this is only a test. We have to at least try. I promise when God say so I will announce it to the world that you are my wife.

I don't know how long Gregg just sat there holding me but when I woke it was dark outside. I watched him sleep and my whole heart melted. He opened his eyes, looked at me and shook his head.

Nicki you are so beautiful. I will never stop telling you that. You are like a drug that I can't get enough of. I would marry you over a thousand times. Please be patient with me. God is not finished with me.

Gregg whatever you want to do, I'll do it.

It's settled then. I'll pick you up for church at ten.

Sunday morning Gregg and Nicki walked in church together and that was the beginning of the charade …

Also My Wife

G regg shook those thoughts off him as his phone began to ring.

Hello Pastor Ron how are you? Is Nicki ok nothing's happened has it?

His heart began to race in his chest.

No son I need to talk to you. I was wondering if you can meet me in my office in an hour.

Sure I can be there.

Gregg hung up and wondered what Pastor Ron wanted with him that was so urgent. He left early so that he wouldn't run into the evening traffic and be late.

Gregg walked into the office and saw Mother Christine seated in front of the desk. She was not looking too happy to see him. His instincts told him that this was not going to be a meeting about church business.

Pastor Ron walked in as Gregg was greeting Mother Christine with a kiss on the cheek.

I'm so glad you could make it. Can I get you something to drink coffee, coke or water?

I'm good Pastor what can I help you with?

Suddenly Christine began shouting at Gregg.

How you could do such a thing with my daughter I will never know!

Pastor Ron hushed her and looked at Gregg.

Son, we got some disturbing news from Nicki's doctor. It seems as though Nicki is not the only one in that room fighting for her life.

Gregg did a double take at Pastor Ron. He wasn't understanding what the man was saying.

There was someone else in the car with Nicki? Who? I was at the hospital and no one said anything about a passenger.

Son I'm saying Nicki is carrying a child. She's pregnant.

Pregnant? Gregg could barely get the word. He was shocked and happy at the same time.

Pastor Ron was talking again but Gregg didn't hear a word he said.

I'm sorry Pastor, but what did you just say?

I said that this has put the church and my family in a difficult situation. I don't know how to proceed from this point. I don't know if I should ask you to step down from your position or ask you your intentions for my daughter.

I looked over at Nicki's mom and she was livid.

My daughter is fighting for her life and I don't even know if she's aware that now she's fighting for her baby also.

I found myself speaking up for Nicki. *Nicki couldn't know that she's having a baby,* I said. *Just what did the doctor say about the baby?*

Pastor Ron was trying to be patient with his young assistant but his patience was fading fast.

The doctor said that if things take a turn for the worse, they will have to abort the baby.

They can't do that. That is my child we are talking about.

Christine spoke up then.

AND THAT IS MY CHILD THAT'S FIGHTING FOR HER LIFE!

Gregg looked at Christine.

Mother Christine that is also my wife. Gregg said through tears. *We have been married for four months now.*

Both Pastor Ron and Mother Christine looked at Gregg as if he were lying. So he continued.

When Nicki and I took that trip to Atlanta there was a Pastor's convention going on at the hotel where we were staying. I asked Nicki to marry me there, she said yes and two Pastors married us. We have been trying to figure out if we should stay married.

Christine looked relieved but not convinced.

Excuse me for a second and I'll go get the license from my car.

Walking out to the car, Gregg thought about his wife and child fighting for their lives and he simply couldn't wait to get to that hospital.

He took the document back in to them, excused himself again and went to be by his wife and child's side.

When We Are Weak

T he ride to the hospital was nerve wrecking. I was sure Nicki didn't know about the baby one minute and the next minute I was sure she did. Nicki wouldn't keep something like that from me, would she?

When I got to Nicki's room Jackie was sitting by the bed holding her hand and talking to her with tears in her eyes. She looked at me as if I had the answers.

She's going to make it right?

Yes. I said, trying to convince myself as well.

Nicki looked so small lying in that bed. The thoughts of her carrying our child almost brought me to my knees. I asked Jackie to give me a second alone with her. Jackie got up and told me that she would be right outside.

I looked down at Nicki and put my hand on her stomach wanting to feel the life that I had created inside of her. I began to pray like I had never prayed before in all my life. I prayed for my unborn child, my wife myself and the time I lost waiting for an answer when the answer had already been given to me.

I cried as I rubbed her stomach. Lord have mercy on us save my family. I lost it in that room that very moment. I fell on my knees and sent up a prayer so powerful that it shook me to my very core. I was so weak that I couldn't stand back up.

Next thing I knew someone was lifting me back to my feet. It was Pastor Ron and Mother Christine. Each had an arm hooked through mine as they helped me to a chair.

I'm so sorry that you two saw my weakness. I thought I was strong.

Son when we are weak God is strong, said Pastor Ron.

We joined hands and Pastor Ron began to pray. When he finished Mother Christine took over and when she finished Jackie prayed.

Pastor Ron's Prayer

Father, all your ways are loving and faithful. We come to you now asking that you be an Intercessor, Healer, Counselor and Comforter. Lord we know that in life there are going to be

trials and difficulties. Good times and tough times. None of us know what life holds, but we know that we need you Lord. We're facing what looks to be an impossible situation but your word teaches us that your ways are not our ways. That you know the plans that you have for us. Lord today we thank you for your faithfulness in the name of Jesus we pray. Amen

Mother Christine's Prayer

Lord, in the name of Jesus, it is to your keeping that I place my child. Knowing that you are able to do exceedingly and abundantly more than I can ever ask for. Thank you for the angels that you've commanded to watch over and guard her so that she will not dash her foot against a stone. You are EL Shaddai, so I know that all things are possible. In Jeremiah you said that the plans you have for us is to prosper us not harm us, plans to give hope and a future. Lord Nicki's future is in your hands right now. Restore her, in Jesus Mighty Name I pray. Amen.

Jackie's Prayer

Lord, hear my voice as I cry out to you for mercy. Thank you for your stable and unchanging nature. Help us to hide ourselves in you. When troubles and confusion comes our way. Remind us that these battles are not ours to fight but yours. We glorify your name and we dare not forget to give glory in the name of Jesus Christ. Amen

Before long everyone was in tears. I looked over at my wife and child fighting for their life and knew that Nicki didn't know that she was carrying our child.

Secrets Revealed

A small voice of doubt tried to convince me that Nicki knew she was pregnant. But then I remembered how sincere she was when she promised never to keep secrets from me again. I believed in my wife.

I looked at everyone in the room who was connected to us one way or another and knew that I had to tell them and not keep it a secret any longer.

I called Rhonda, Ryan and Monica. I wanted everyone to be here when I told the story. It took everyone only twenty minutes to get there.

After we were all seated, I stood up and confessed to them mines and Nicki's sin and asked for their forgiveness. I told them about the marriage, the separation and now the baby.

Everybody was shocked. No one spoke for a long time and then everyone began to talk at once.

When did yall get married? Rhonda asked.

When we went to Atlanta we both decided the time was right. We really bonded there – walking, talking, seeing sights and eating meals together. We talked about family and friends and just decided that the time was right. We knew that if we included you all it would be a long way away, with everyone's plans so we decided we didn't want to wait and the rest is history.

I really felt bad for not telling the whole story but now was not the place or the time'. Jackie came over and hugged me.

As long as we are sharing secrets I may as well tell you all that Sherman and I have been seeing each other for over a year and we got engaged tonight. This is a bitter sweet moment for me, while there is joy in my heart there is also sadness too, Jackie said through tears.

It's going to be alright baby, Sherman came to her and hugged her tight.

Monica decided to share some good news to lighten the mood.

I will finally open my own real estate firm. I'm waiting for the deal to close but I have faith that God will provide, she said and began to cry.

Look everyone Nicki is a fighter, Ryan said. *Do you all remember when she had that accident on route 66? Nobody believed that anyone walked away from that accident but Nicki did! Not even a scratch. No broken bones or nothing. I believe that Nicki and the baby will pull through this. Now do anyone else have anything else they want to confess?*

Monica nodded slowly, *I'm going to be an aunt.* Then she burst into tears.

Nobody else said anything after that, but Gregg had a feeling that the real skeletons were going to fall out closets soon!

Sherman's Secret

At the office, Sherman was dealing with his own demons. A few years ago he had made the mistake of taking out one of his clients on a date. The way he rationalized it was that Jackie would never know because it was just a one night stand.

But now, he was being harassed. She was calling him at the office, at home and on his cell phone. She wouldn't let go. Sherman cursed the day he'd ever said hello to Jenny. She now stood in the way of his happiness.

At the end of his rope, feeling like there was nowhere left to turn, he looked up to Heaven and pleaded with God to forgive him for his selfish ways.

He knew that real soon he was going to have to tell Jackie before she found out from someone else. Sherman didn't want to hurt her nor did he want to lose her.

His cell phone began to vibrate. He looked down at it and saw Jenny's number on the screen.

Will you please stop calling me?

I need to see you tonight.

I can't I have too much work to get done before the end of the month.

Jenny was silent for a while but then she spoke with conviction.

Either you see me tonight or I come to your house and sleep on you doorsteps.

Sherman knew that he had no choice but to agree to see her because Jenny had proved that she did not make idol threats.

He thought about getting a restraining order against her but realized he'd have to confess the situation to his Uncle Dale who was a police officer. Uncle Dale and his sister, Sherman's mom, didn't keep secrets from each other. Sherman agreed to meet her at a bar right outside of town where he knew he wouldn't run into anyone he knew.

He took his time driving to the bar and when he arrived, Jenny waved him over to the table where she was sitting at. His stomach turned over causing his face to frown as he made his way toward what was becoming the nightmare that held his fate in her hands.

Hey baby. I'm so glad you could make it, I've missed you. How have you been?

Sherman remembered a scripture that was read in church last Sunday that said *let us come boldly to the throne of grace that we may obtain mercy and find grace to help in the time of need.*

He looked up and thought, *Lord if this is not the time of need I don't know when. I am sitting here in a storm I have created asking you to bring me out of it.*

So what was so important that you needed to see me about?

Jenny smiled and then asked the waiter for a drink menu. After her drink arrived she took a sip and started to talk about how much she loved and missed him.

Sherman knew he had to at least try to get through to her that this was not what she thought it was.

Jenny I need to say some things to you and I need you to listen and try to understand what I'm saying. I don't love you. I am not in love with you. I made a mistake taking you out. Please stop calling, texting and coming to my job. I don't want to be in a relationship with you. I am not your man nor will I ever be. Forgive me.

Jenny looked at Sherman with tears in her eyes.

What's wrong with me? Why don't you love me? You made love to me. You enjoyed that night. You couldn't wait for me to undress. You were all over me and now you tell me it meant nothing. How am I supposed to feel? Should I be happy you used me? You want me to just walk away and let you be happy? I don't think so. You are going to treat me like I deserve to be treated. We are a couple now. I will expect to be wined and dined and pampered like you loved me. Until you start to do those things I will stalk you everywhere you go.

I looked at her like she had grown two heads and I don't know what came over me but I started to laugh until my sides began to hurt.

So you think this is funny?

No I didn't mean to laugh but I know you can't be that crazy to think that you can make someone do something that they have no intention of doing. Look, I said that I'm sorry and now I'm going to get up and walk out that door the same way I walked in without you and if you ever come near me again I will have you arrested do I make myself clear?

Jenny looked hard at Sherman.

You will regret this.

She got up and walked out of the bar.

Sherman didn't know if he was relieved or scared.

God's Glory

S herman made it to his car, got inside and just sat there. He thought maybe he should call Jackie and tell her everything but then what if she left him? He couldn't bear the thought of Jackie not being in his life. He had messed up big time.

Maybe if I slept on it I would see things differently in the morning.

With that being said, Sherman drove home, showered and got into bed. An hour later he was still tossing and turning so he got up, got out his bible and began to search the scriptures to find out if maybe he could figure this out for himself.

Two hours later, he was still reading the bible and realizing that he didn't know God at all.

I never thought that I was saved but I did think that I knew who God was and that he knew me.

All the knowledge in the world had not prepare him for what God was saying to him as he read chapter after chapter of His word. Sherman knew at that moment that he needed to be born again. He was the worst kind of sinner.

God is in control of my life and I know that he loves me at this very hour.

Tears began to rundown his face as he accepted Christ right where he was kneeling beside his bed. Sherman knew then that he had to humble himself under the mighty hand of God.

Sherman realized that God had allowed him to go through this light affliction because He had a bigger and better plan for his life. This testing was for his good and God's glory.

The Prodigal Son

F inally Sherman fell asleep and was awakened by the sunlight coming through his window when he opened his eyes.

After work he called Jenny but she wouldn't answer her phone. He didn't want to talk to Jackie until he'd had the chance to talk to Jenny one more time so he drove over to his mom's house hoping that he could talk to her about the mess he had gotten himself in.

The smile on his mom's face was priceless. Chiante was truly happy to see her son. Together they walked through her spacious home to the kitchen where she was preparing something that smelled delicious.

I know that smell, that's a Santé Fe southwestern omelet with green peppers and onions - my favorite. I said, suddenly realizing how hungry I was.

Yes it is. I'm so glad you stopped by. You look like you could use a home cooked meal. Is something wrong? You look like you lost your friend.

Let's eat and I'll tell you about it over breakfast.

Sherman felt his mom was the greatest mom in the world. His dad died when he was fourteen and Chiante made sure that her son got a good education, kept him on track and made sure he knew how proud of him she was. Sherman's mom was a Judge in the Dade County area and her brother, Dale made sure Sherman became the man his father could be proud of.

No sooner had Sherman thought of his Uncle Dale, the doorbell rang. Mom excused herself to see who was at the door and walked back in with Uncle Dale who was still in his police uniform. He fixed himself a plate and sat down next to Sherman.

The prodigal son returns. Chiante and I were just talking about you yesterday. What brings you here other than the good food?

Uncle Dale thought he knew me so well.

I wanted to talk to mom but I'm glad you are here too.

Uh oh, what have you gotten into now? Your mom was just saying she thought something was going on with you.

Mom has always had this sixth sense when it came to me.

Sherman stole a quick look at his mom and started talking.

Last year I met this woman as I was leaving the office. She was cute, so I decided to say hi. I walked over introduced myself to her, got her phone number and started to call and talk to her. Jackie was busy with her studies and I wasn't seeing much of her and I got lonely. After a couple of months of talking on the phone, I asked her out on a date. She was funny and a month later I slept with her.

Chiante shook her head.

Is she pregnant?

Sherman didn't know which was worse – pregnant or crazy.

No mom she's not but she is crazy. She's started stalking me and now she has threatened me too. I met her last night to try to reason with her and it didn't work. I've asked Jackie to marry me and she said yes and now this lady is trying to destroy me.

Chiante exchanged looks with her brother and told her son to sit. For a few seconds she said nothing and just stared at Sherman.

I raised you to be honest, have you been honest with Jackie about this?

Sherman shook his head no.

The first thing you've got to do is tell Jackie about her and let her decide if you are the man that she wants to spend the rest of her life with. You know that this is going to be hard for her and it's going to take time for her to process this. You have nobody to blame but yourself.

As we were talking Uncle Dale's phone rung and he excused himself to answer it. A few minutes later he came back in the room and said that there had been a homicide and he had to go.

Mom and I stood there in shock watching him leave. Homicides didn't happen often in their small town.

Chiante said a quick prayer for the victim and their family. Then she returned her attention to her son.

Look Sherman I know that this does not look like it's going to work itself out but trust God and it will. You've done crazier things in the past and somehow they worked out so stop worrying so much and let's eat.

Chiante and her son talked for a while and then she walked him to the door, kissed him goodbye and Sherman headed to work.

On the way he sent up a small prayer hoping that today would be a better day.

In A Split Second

Sherman arrived to his office and decided to call Jackie to see how her day was going and to tell her how much he loved her.

Hey baby I just wanted to hear your voice.

Jackie had a way of making him feel like he was the best thing that ever happened to her.

I'm good baby just have to get through my finals and then I can spend some quality time with you. You know I love you so much and I miss spending time with you?

I know sometimes it gets lonely without you. I know but after this week I'm all yours.

We can start to plan our wedding. Have you heard anything about Nicki?

No I haven't talked to Gregg today but I'm going by after school today.

Ok I'll meet you at the hospital I told her. Ace that test and I'll see you later.

After he hung up, Sherman was smiling so hard his secretary asked him had he hit the lottery.

Later that morning, Sherman called Gregg to see if he could meet him for lunch. He needed a man of God's point of view on what to do about Jenny.

Gregg didn't want to leave the hospital so Sherman told him he would come to the hospital because he really needed to talk to him.

Sherman realized that Nicki's condition hadn't changed much because worry was all over Greggs face.

Man I know that this is hard for you but she's going to be ok. I just know it.

Gregg kissed Nicki and the two men left the room and headed to the waiting area. No one was there they we sat down.

What's on your mind Sherman? Something is bothering you I can tell.

As Sherman started to open his mouth to speak something on the TV monitor caught his attention. The news guy was breaking a story about a murder in the apartment complex where Jenny lived. As Sherman watched the story break, EMTs were coming out of Jenny's apartment with someone in a black body bag.

Sherman's heart was in his throat and suddenly he couldn't breathe.

Gregg, something bad has happened the home of a girl that I came here to talk to you about.

What are you talking about Sherman? I thought you and Jackie were engaged. Now you're sitting here looking like you've seen a ghost and telling me you were seeing someone else?

No, man. Look, I had a one night stand with this chick a couple of months ago and now she won't leave me alone. I came here to talk to you about it before I talked to Jackie. I tried to tell her last night that I didn't want her and what happened between us was a mistake but she wouldn't listen. She told me that she was going to make my life a living hell and I believe she will. I don't know why I went there with her, maybe I was lonely because Jackie was studying so much or maybe I thought she was cute and I wanted to flirt. I don't know but it happened and now I can't get rid of her. I don't know what else to do man. I know that I have to tell Jackie and I don't know how to tell her. I thought maybe you had a word for me. I don't know what just happened in her apartment but whatever it was it was bad. Look man I've got to go. I'll call you later.

Sherman rushed from the hospital waiting area and out of the hospital in a daze. He didn't know where to go. He wanted to go to Jenny's to make sure she was alright but everything in him told him to go back to the office so he headed back there. He parked my car in the underground parking garage and walked across the street in deep thought.

When he got back to his office, his Uncle Dale was there waiting for him.

Where have you been? Uncle Dale asked him.

I've been to the hospital talking with Gregg

Sit down. I need to talk to you.

Sherman's heart began to beat so loud he was afraid his Uncle would hear it.

Sherman there has been a murder at that girl's apartment that you were seeing. Sometime last night or early this morning someone murdered her. I have to ask you did you do it. I know you saw her last night. You told us about meeting her having dinner and you said that she walked out making threats to ruin you. I don't want to think the worst but you have to know that you're a suspect in her murder. Did you at any time go to her apartment last night or this morning?

Uncle Dale I promise you she was alive and well when she walked out of that restaurant. I didn't talk to her after that.

I have to ask you to come with me down to the station for questioning.

Sherman's heart sank to his toes.

I did not kill her. I could never do that. You know me. You know I am innocent.

I know son, but we have to follow procedures. I will call your mom to meet us there.

In a split second Sherman's life was changed forever. All he could think about was Jackie and that she would never marry him now.

Only God Knows

During the drive downtown, Uncle Dale kept asking Sherman the same questions over and over. Sherman thought to himself that this has got to be a nightmare.

Did anyone see you come in or go out of your house last night?

No Uncle Dale. Only God knows.

At the station Sherman was put in a tiny room with two chairs and a table. He didn't know where Uncle Dale had disappeared too. He was in that room for an hour before another officer walked through the door and introduced himself as detective Monroe. He was a large man with a tired looking face, like he had seen too much in his life to ever talk about.

I need to ask you a few questions son about Jenny Thomas. The first question is how do you know her and second, what is your relationship to her.

Sherman looked at Detective Monroe. He knew the law well.

It this where I say I need a lawyer?

You have every right to a lawyer. I'm asking you to cooperate with us as you are only a person of interest right now. You have not been charged with anything. If you think you need a lawyer you can request one.

Sherman thought about it for a few seconds and he knew that he hadn't done anything to harm anyone so he told the detective what he'd told Uncle Dale.

I called her last night to see if I could talk sense into her and she didn't answer the phone. I went this morning to my mother's home to talk to her about the situation and I left her home drove to work, left for lunch and drove to the hospital to talk to a friend to see if he had any suggestions and while I was there I saw on the news a body being carried out of Jenny's apartment. I left the hospital went back to work and that's when I found out that it was Jenny. I could never hurt anyone. I met her a few months back, we went out a couple of times I had sex with her once, broke it off and now this. I met her for a drink at Dell's bar and grill and she threaten to make my life a living hell before she left me sitting at the bar. The bartender can tell you that I didn't leave with her nor did I go to her home after I left the bar. And no one saw me come home because I live alone.

Detective Malone looked at Sherman, stopped the recorder which was sitting on the table and walked out the room leaving Sherman sitting there looking crazy.

Every thought imaginable was going through his mind. Did he believe Him? Who would have wanted to kill Jenny? Would Sherman be blamed for it? Will they come back and arrest him? But most of all, what will Jackie think of this mess that he had gotten myself into?

Twenty minutes went by before the door opened again and Uncle Dale stepped in the room.

Come on son, let's go home.

Sherman was holding his breath and didn't realize it until he broke down and cried on Uncle Dale's shoulder.

It's going to be alright son. You just cannot leave the state until this is over. Dry your eyes because Chiante is waiting in the lobby.

As Sherman and his Uncle Dale passed room after room, he saw Detective Monroe standing in the last room. Sherman knew he didn't want to ever see him again.

Trials and Tribulations

Chiante threw her arms around her son's neck and kissed his cheeks and started to cry. The three of them walked out to her car and Sherman got in. Chiante and her brother had a private conversation while Sherman sat numb on the inside.

On the drive to his mom's home, Sherman told her the same things he had told Uncle Dale and the detective.

Once inside her home, Chiante told her son she thought he needed a lawyer.

I don't think I do. I did not kill anyone and I don't know who did.

Just to be on the safe side I think I'll retain one. I know you're not a murderer but I don't want you to end up back there again.

Mom I think we should just wait and see what uncle Dale has to say about this. I need to call Jackie and tell her about this before she hears it on the news. I should have told her months ago. I'm just worried she will walk away forever and I don't think I can take that.

Ok baby you do what you think is best.

Sherman dialed Jackie's number, waited for her to pick up and felt his heart beat a mile a minute.

Hello this is Jackie I can't take your call right now. Leave a message and I'll get back to you shortly.

Damn her answering machine.

Sherman left Jackie a message and went to find his mom.

What did she say?

Nothing her machine was on, so I left a message and if she hears it she'll be here at seven. If not I'll go to her.

What if she decides that you were being dishonest with her and the whole relationship has been a lie? Then what?

I haven't thought that. I was planning to tell her everything, ask for her forgiveness and hopefully move forward.

Sherman sometimes life is not as simple as we would like it to be. There are trials and tribulations on this journey. Maybe I sheltered you too long. I'm just saying that I'm a woman first and if you were my future husband and something like this happened to the man that I was going to marry I would have to question his character. I wouldn't be able to just forget and forgive that easy. First of all you cheated on her then you kept on talking to the person you cheated with for over six months. And now you want her to believe that you love her and this will never happen again. I wouldn't believe that. I would have to walk away so be prepared for Jackie to walk away. You have to learn that trust is priceless and once it's lost it's hard to regain.

More Than He's Saying

Jackie was leaving school. It was her last class before finally graduating and she'd planned on dropping by the hospital to check on Nicki when her cell phone vibrated. She looked down and saw a missed call from Sherman and smiled as she got in the car.

Maybe he wants to celebrate tonight because that's what she felt like doing. She had passed all her finals and now she was officially finished with school. It felt good!

As she waited for the car to cool off she listened to his message.

Hey babe I need to talk to you as soon as possible. I'm at moms so if you can come by around seven if you're not here by seven, I'll drop by your house.

Jackie thought that was strange that he would give a time limit but maybe he just wanted to surprise her with something since he knew it was her last day of school. He was so thoughtful and sweet. She looked at her watch and noticed it was only four so she had plenty of time to stop at the hospital and make it to Chiante's house before seven.

When Jackie walked into Nicki's room Gregg was sitting by the bed reading the bible to a still unconscious Nicki. She wanted to cry but instead she walked over to the bed, leaned in and gave Nicki a kiss on the forehead.

Jackie hugged Gregg and asked if there were any changes. He shook his head no but said that her vitals were getting stronger and he still believed that the God he served was still working things out.

How are you doing?

I passed my finals and I couldn't be happier. Now I can start to focus more on Sherman and I.

He dropped by earlier and something was on the news that caught his eye so he left.

Oh yea what was it?

I just saw the end part about a murder and he left. It's almost time for the news you want to watch and see if they say something about it again?

Sure why not, I don't have to meet him for a while.

As Jackie and Gregg watched the news, they saw the police emerging from an apartment building and people standing around. The newsman was saying that the girl that lived there was murdered and that a person of interest was being questioned.

Jackie watched Sherman's Uncle Dale come down the steps with a lady who she didn't know beside him.

Do you know anyone who lives in that building?

No when we first moved here we checked out those apartments because they had security on site but we decided to buy a home instead.

Maybe Sherman knew someone who lived there. I don't know but I'm about to find out.

Jackie got up, kissed Nicki good night and told Gregg she'd stop by tomorrow. On the drive over she wondered what Gregg knew about the murder. Something inside of her told her that he knew more than he was saying.

A Thousand Pieces

Jackie parked in the drive behind Uncle Dale's car and walked the short distance to the house all the while her mind was trying to figure out what Gregg knew.

She rang the doorbell and soon Chiante opened the door, kissed her on the cheek and offered her inside in her beautiful home. Sherman was standing in the kitchen talking to Uncle Dale. He shut up as I entered the room which was strange to me but I smiled and gave him a kiss and hugged Uncle Dale.

There was a moment when no one said anything and then everybody was trying to talk at once. We all laughed and then Dale and Chiante excused themselves from the room.

Babe I need to talk to you about something. I need you to hear me out before you speak so please sit down or would you like to talk in the den?

No, here is fine.

While he was getting his thoughts together I was having thoughts of my own like, Why hadn't he mentioned my finishing school or better still why didn't he ask me if I had passed or not. I knew then that what he was about to tell me would be bad.

Do you remember when you started school and you were so busy?

I just gave him a slight nod.

I would always tell you that I was feeling neglected, but you would just brush me off and say that I was being dramatic. Well I met this girl and I thought that I could just take her out and we could just be friends. It didn't work out that way. I asked her out we went to a bar, I got a little too drunk and we went back to her place and you can imagine the rest. Next day I realized I had made a big mistake and told her I couldn't see her any more. I told her that I was in a relationship. She didn't like it but I promise you I didn't go back there. I didn't see her again until a month ago when she started calling my office and following me around and making trouble for me. Two days ago she called and threaten me so I met her at Stacy's and tried to have a conversation with her. It didn't go well and she told me that I couldn't just use her and walk away. She said she would make sure everyone knew about us. I walked away and never looked back. I know I was wrong. I was just feeling lonely and I wanted someone to talk to and she seemed like a nice lady. Babe I'm sorry that I cheated on you. I'm asking you to forgive me. Please forgive me.

Jackie sat still. She was stunned. Tears were running down her face as she listened to the man she loved with all my heart tell her he had cheated on her and he still was not through with the story.

Yesterday morning I came here to tell mom what I had done and to get advice on how to tell you and she was willing to help me out so I went to the hospital to talk to Gregg and before I could tell him I saw on the news that someone had been murdered in the same building that she lived in so I left and went back to the office so I could figure this out and as I pulled up Uncle Dale pulled up to take me down to headquarters to question me for her murder. I'm telling you I didn't do it - like I told him. My life right now is in a mess. Please don't leave me now. I need you more than anything now.

Sherman finished talking but Jackie still couldn't say anything. It was like someone had sucker punched her in her gut. She looked at him and it was as if she didn't know him anymore.

She couldn't speak. Hell, she couldn't even think. In a daze, she somehow managed to get to her car. Jackie was crying so hard she could hardly see where she was going.

Her cell phone was ringing all the way home but she didn't bother to see who was calling because she already knew. In the safety of her home, Jackie sat on the couch waiting on God to say something or whisper something in my ear but all she heard was the sound of her own heart breaking into a thousand pieces.

She could not believe that Sherman would think that she would consider staying with a man who was unfaithful. GG would not hear of it. She would say if he cheated once he'll do it again.

Jackie needed to talk to Nicki but that was impossible. She knew if she called GG she would comfort her and then give her advice that she already knew deep inside of her. She started to pray and asked God to answer her quick, fast, and in a hurry.

The Whole Armor

S herman started to run after Jackie, but Uncle Dale grabbed his arm and pulled him back.

I can't let you go after her. Son, let her calm down.

Sherman's heart was beating so fast he thought it would burst.

Uncle Dale you don't understand. I have to talk to her. She listened to me and never said a word. No anger- just tears. No slap in the face- just tears.

I know son. That's when you know a woman is really hurt, when she says nothing and just walks away. But you've got to give her a little time. You just dropped a huge bomb on her. I can't let you go over to her house you are already in enough trouble.

I need to talk to her. She won't answer her phone. I need to explain to her how much I love her. I can't lose her. I just can't.

Chiante hated to see her only child going through so much pain. She walked over and hugged him.

Come sit down. Let's try to figure this thing out.

We were sitting side by side when she looked me in my eye and asked me a hard question.

What you would have done if the situation were reversed.

The question threw Sherman. He honestly didn't know.

I would never believe that Jackie would cheat on me.

That's where she's at now. She never thought you would either. Her feelings are all over the place. Now you have to wait to see if she will forgive you. I know that you're in a lot of pain now but she's in more, you cheated and the girl is dead and you are a suspect, you dropped all that on a person that you're suppose to marry. My God son you have got to give her time to sort this out. It's ok to leave her messages but she doesn't want to see you right now. This is where your faith comes in, the word tells you to put on the whole armor of God so that when the day of evil comes you may be able to stand your ground and after you have done everything stand. I am not dismissing what you did because you were wrong, I truly believe you love her but you have a lot on your plate right now and I think you should go up to the guest room and rest. I want you to stay here tonight.

Uncle Dale agreed with his sister so Sherman went upstairs to bed. After a hot shower, he got on his knees to talk to God.

Her Eyes Were Open

Gregg was sitting by the bed reading the bible when he looked over in the bed that Nicki was laying in and to his surprise her eyes was open! He jumped up and spoke to her.

Nicki can you hear me? Do you know who I am? Stay right here don't move.

He was scared to leave her but he had to get the nurse or the doctor or somebody.

Gregg started yelling for someone and both the doctor and nurse came out of the nurse station to see what was going on.

She's up! I mean her eyes are open. She nodded at me so I think she understands me.

He was rambling and so. He just wanted them to hurry up and get in the room. The doctor and the nurse stepped into the room and sure enough Nicki's eyes were still opened and she was trying to talk but since she had be in an unconscious state for so long her voice was low and no one couldn't understand anything she was trying to say.

Gregg was certain that Nicki knew who he was and that a miracle was unfolding before his eyes!

They asked him to step out of the room for a while so they could exam her. Gregg immediately started calling everyone. First her parents, then Jackie and his sister Rhonda.

Pastor picked up on the first ring and after Gregg told him about Nicki, they told him they were on their way.

Jackie sounded strange but she was on her way also. He couldn't get Rhonda but he did reach Chiante and she too said she was on her way.

Chiante peeked into the room where Sherman was kneeling in prayer, watched her son cry out to God and then gently closed the door and left without disturbing him.

On the way to the hospital Chiante took the time to talk to God.

God I know that my son is not a saint nor is he a bad child. I'm asking you to give him what you see that he needs right now. Let the police find the killer of that young lady because I know in my heart that my son could not have hurt her. Fix us and thank you for healing, in Jesus name. Amen.

Christine was getting out of the car when Chiante arrived. The two friends embraced each other and walked in together.

The nurse came out into the hallway and led us all to a waiting room until the doctor could come and talk to us.

Jackie walked in a few seconds later.

Honey what's wrong, you look horrible. Christine asked.

Jackie started crying and allowed Christine to pull her into her embrace.

Nicki will be alright. Gregg called and said she was weak but she knew him and she knew what the doctor was asking her.

Jackie shook her head.

That's great news but that's not why I'm upset. We will talk later. Jackie managed between sobs.

Chiante watched Jackie and Christine in the corner exchanging words and she felt guilty knowing that her son was causing so much pain. Twenty minutes later the doctor came and got Mother Christine and Pastor Ron.

The only ones left in the room were Jackie and Chiante. Chiante walked over to Jackie and hugged her.

Can we talk about what happened earlier?

Jackie nodded her head yes.

I know that what my son did was wrong and I wouldn't begin to try and justify it as being anything else. Take as much time as you need to process and get through this situation. I can tell you that Sherman does love you and he knows that he messed up and I am praying that you two get through this.

Jackie nodded her head again. She had no words and could only cry.

Gregg came into the room and told Jackie that Nicki wanted to see her. Jackie dried her eyes and went to see her best friend.

Nicki was sitting up in bed watching everyone with tears in their eyes and thanking God for her recovery. The doctors had given her an MRI to make sure the swelling had went down in her brain and they had checked her eyes , and reflexes and had sent her to CT and every test came back positive. It had been nothing less than a miracle.

Jackie was standing in the room catching Nicki up on everything that had happened since the accident.

I'm just so glad to see you awake and to know that you remember me. I've missed you and I can't help but give God the praise. He did what no man could. I love you girl.

I love you too! Nicki said slowly.

I'm going to go home and give you and Gregg some time to talk.

Every one said their goodbyes and left Gregg and Nicki. Gregg kept staring at Nicki for signs or clues that she knew about the baby. He wasn't sure how to tell her so he just blurted it out.

Nicki baby, there is something you need to know. Gregg said with excitement. *Sweetheart, you're carrying our child.*

Finding Balance

icki couldn't believe what she'd heard. *What! That can't be true.*

Baby, feel your stomach. Feel the way your waist has expanded. You, Mrs. Howard are with child and you will be having our little boy or girl in a few short months. The baby is fine and so far healthy.

Nicki could not believe that she was pregnant. She tried to get up out of the bed but, Gregg held her there.

Trust me baby you are pregnant. The doctor says maybe tomorrow you can get up and begin moving around.

Just how long have I been here?

Nicki started firing question after question at Gregg and he tried to answer them as fast and as best he could. She remembered everything up to the wreck but nothing after it of course.

The two talked well into the night until she was exhausted. Gregg stepped out of the room and went down the hallway to the chapel and began to give God all the praise he had in him. He knew that he served an awesome God.

J ackie woke up in the middle of the night and went into the kitchen to get a glass of water. Sitting at the table she began to cry once again.

I never thought that I would be like this. Lord what am I going to do? Do I still love Sherman? Could I ever trust him again? My grandmother always said that you may not understand someone, but you don't have to understand them to love them. That's why it's called unconditional love. Right now I'm wondering if this is my test. I know that I've been faithful and I know that I love Sherman still but I know that I don't trust him anymore so do I stay in his life or do I walk away? God please help me, when I talk to him again I want to know that whatever I've decided that I can live with it. This is my prayer.

Jackie sat at that table until she saw the sun peeping out from the clouds and she still didn't have an answer. She went upstairs, got her shower, put on her clothes and headed out to the hospital to see her best friend.

Nicki and Jackie had been friends forever and now Jackie needed to talk to her. She arrived just in time to see Nicki take her first step since the accident. The roundness under her gown was evidence that her pregnancy was coming along just fine.

Jackie knew that Nicki was going to be a great mother. If God allowed her to live and the baby to live then everything was going to be fine.

Gregg was obviously beside himself with joy and as Jackie watched him she noticed that he had lost weight and he was looking tired so she offered to stay with Nicki while he went home to get some much needed rest. He protested at first but finally agreed.

The nurse and Jackie got Nicki back to bed and settled down and then she left the two of them alone.

You look good Nicki. I was so worried about you and you know everyone was praying for you.

I'm humbled that so many people took the time out to pray for me.

Of course. You know everyone loves Nicki!

Speaking of love. Girl Gregg told me you were engaged to Sherman and you two were making wedding plans. I am so happy for you. But you don't look like a woman with a fresh new college degree AND an engagement ring, so out with it. I know something else is going on.

Jackie looked at her best friend and told herself that she wouldn't cry again. She told Nicki everything Sherman told her including the murder.

I watched as all those emotions played over my friend's face then disgust took a permanent stand on her face and I knew then that I wouldn't take Sherman back.

Nicki looked at me hard.

Life is about balance. Be kind, but don't let people abuse you. Trust, but don't be deceived. Be content but never stop improving yourself. What Sherman has done was disrespectful to you but it's up to you to forgive him and move on. If you stay angry with him, he still has power over you to hurt you at any given time. So forgive him and move forward. You've been hurt and now it's time to take care of yourself. What he did to you was unbelievable, I thought he loved you. I see your pain and I know that you are stronger than you think you are so hold on to that inner strength and walk into your destiny.

Nicki I'm hurting so bad right now.

I know Jackie but you are stronger than you think. Don't let your feelings get in the way of your thinking. The deepest level of worship is praising God in spite of the pain. At your lowest, God is your hope, at your darkest God is your light, at your weakest God is your strength, and at your saddest, God is your comforter. We will get through this together like we've always done in the past.

This is not an ending, it's a beginning. Letting go of the wrong person in your life opens doors for the right person to walk in. I'm living proof of that. If God did it for me I know that he will do it for you. Dry your eyes and come give me a hug.

I got up and gave Nicki a hug.

When did you get so smart?

We both laughed and hugged some more. I stayed at the hospital catching her up on everything that had happened while she was unconscious and getting on to her for not telling me about what was going on with her and Gregg. We both agreed not to keep secrets anymore.

Killer Instinct

Around lunch, Sherman stepped in the room and we both turned and stared at him. He kind of stammered and finally he got composed enough to walk into the room.

Hello Jackie. How are you Nicki? I heard that you were awake and I just wanted to stop by.

Nicki spoke first.

Thank-you for stopping by Sherman. I'm feeling good. Just a little tired. Gregg went home for a while but I'll tell him you stopped by.

Yea, thanks.

Then he looked straight at me.

Jackie can I have a word with you outside?

I started to tell him that we had nothing to talk about but when I looked over at Nicki she nodded her head so I said sure.

We stepped in the hall and he grabbed for me and I stepped back.

Don't touch me, what's your problem? Just say what you have to say and leave.

Sherman looked at me and backed up.

I never meant to hurt you. I love you. I want to marry you. Please don't give up on me. I will admit that I made a big mistake with that girl but you have to believe that it meant nothing, nothing at all. Tell me you believe me Jackie. Tell me that you will give me a second chance. Please tell me that you still love me.

He looked so pitiful that I almost was convinced that he deserved a second chance then a thought popped in my head and reminded me that if he loved me, he would not have cheated. I looked at the man that I was suppose to marry and love 'til death do us part.

I love you with all my heart but you thought that my love wasn't enough so you went out cheated and now you stand here hoping that I'll forgive you and take you back. I do forgive you but I can't take you back. I just can't. I turned and walked back in the room.

My heart was beating so fast. I knew Sherman was going to cause a scene but when I looked back he was walking away. Nicki was sitting up in bed looking like she wanted to cry.

I'm sorry about that I hope we didn't upset you?

No girl, are you alright?

Yes I'll be ok. I'm just glad you're here for me.

Sherman didn't know what else to do he knew that what he was doing wouldn't bring Jackie back. When he returned to the office his Uncle Dale was waiting for him.

Hey you look down. I've got some news that I think will perk you back up. Jenny had an ex who had been tracking her for over two years. We caught up with him when he tried to use her credit card at an ATM in Georgia. He confessed to everything and now he's being extradited back to Florida. You dodged a bullet son because Detective Moody was convinced it was you. Now that's something to shout about.

Uncle Dale was so happy but Sherman couldn't even smile. He hit me on the back and told me that he knew that killing was not in my nature. But he was wrong. I had killed Jackie's love.

Lemons & Lemonade

Jackie was sitting by her pool just staring out into the distance. Remembering what it was like for her to give her heart to Sherman to completely stomp it to the ground. She hated going through crap like this. She hated the idea that he screwed another girl while he was with her. She also knew if he did it once he would do it again and now her world had been turned upside down and she had to figure a way to fix it.

God I can't even seem to hear from you.

As a tear rolled down her cheek she brushed it away with determination.

I will not cry. I did nothing wrong and everything right.

Her phone was ringing as she looked down and saw her boss's number pop up on her caller ID.

Hello. Yes Mr. Findley this is Jackie.

After their brief conversation, Jackie jumped up and began to give God the praise. She did a little dance around the pool and the grin on her face was as big as the Mississippi river. Her Granny always said when the world gives you lemons make lemonade and that's what she was going to do.

She rushed upstairs, packed a suitcase, showered and changed so quick you would have thought her house was on fire. Jackie got to the airport in record time. Gloria, Mr. Findley's assistant, was waiting at the gate with their tickets. As they boarded the plane Jackie knew that she had made the right decision.

***

G regg was still so amazed by Nicki's progress that he could only stare at his wife in wonder. He walked over to the bed and gave her a big kiss. She looked at him and smiled.

I was so worried about you and the baby I almost lost it.

It's over now baby we are fine.

I know you are and for the rest of my life I will be there for the both of you.

The doctor walked in with a big smile on his face.

I've got great news for you, if all your test comes back normal you can go home tomorrow.

Both Gregg and Nicki were so happy. After the doctor left Nicki looked at Gregg and asked him, where is home for me and the baby?

I've already moved all of your stuff into my home while you were here. I hope you don't mind?

Oh baby you have made me one of the happiest women in the world.

At that moment Gregg knew in his heart that he and Nicki would be just fine.

S herman decided to go by Jackie's house on his way home. He stopped by the florist first and picked up her favorite roses and thought about what he would say to her. He hoped she would be ready to hear what he had to say. He knew that he could convince her to take him back.

He parked in her drive way and noticed her car was not there so he decided to wait for her on the porch. Sherman waited until one in the morning and was getting more worried by the minute.

Where could she be?

He thought maybe she'd gone to Granny's, so he rode by her house but her car wasn't there. There was nowhere else she would be at this time of night so he rode back by her house and her car still wasn't there. Now he was alarmed. He couldn't go home so he parked in her driveway to wait on her. He must have dosed off because when he woke it was six in the morning, and she still hadn't come home.

He finally left feeling disappointed and hurt. Sherman drove home, showered and tried to call Jackie's cell to no avail.

Where was she?

On his way in to work, Sherman had stopped by the hospital to see if Jackie was there with Nicki only to find out that she'd been discharged. He then went to Gregg's house. Gregg answered the door and looked surprised to see Sherman.

After asking about Nicki and the baby, he got right to the point.

Have you or Nicki seen Jackie since yesterday?

No she left after I got back to the hospital. Said she was going home. Why, what's up?

I've looked everywhere and it's like she has dropped off the face of the earth.

Come on in and I'll see if she's talked to Nicki.

Gregg came back down the steps and told him that Nicki said she hadn't talked to Jackie since yesterday.

She won't answer her phone and now I'm worried.

Have you talked to her granny?

Yes and she haven't talked to her either and she's not at work.

Maybe you should talk to Dale.

That's my next stop. He's at my mom's place.

New Beginnings & Goodbyes

Sherman walked in my mother's house feeling so down and not knowing what to do. One look at him and Chiante rushed over and gave her son a big hug.

Baby sit down I have to talk to you.

Sherman sat down on the couch and she pulled him to her just like she use to do when he was younger.

I talked to Jackie last night and she wanted me to tell you that she took a position away from here and that she wouldn't be coming back, she had to get away from this town. Her granny and some friends will be packing her house up and an agent will put it up for sale, she doesn't want you to look for her because she say's it's over. I don't want you to worry about this, stress about this, or try to figure this out, I simply want you to pray about it and let it go, you went about it the wrong way and that got you where you are today so now I want you to let her go because she does not want to talk to you or see you right now. I know this is going to be hard but if you love her you have to let her go.

Sherman turned toward his mother and cried like he was seven years old. He failed to see the hurt in her eyes as she rocked him.

N icki had just dosed off when her cell phone rang. It was Jackie calling.

Girl, where are you?

I'm in Georgia, Atlanta to be exact. I was beginning to get depressed and starting to doubt God when my boss called and offered me the executive position in the Georgia office and it comes with the penthouse and all the amenities. I didn't think. I just said yes and the view is beautiful. I met my team this morning and I know that everything is going to work out for my good. I will be back for you when the baby is born and GG is packing up my house along with all our friends so pray for me.

Are you sure this is what you want? Don't let him run you out of town.

Yes Nic I'm sure. If I had stayed there I would have taken him back and I know in my heart that I could not forgive him being that close to him. Be happy for me, I'm going to need you more now than I ever have.

Ok I love you Jackie. I just want what's best for you.

I'll be back to visit and now you and the baby can visit me. I've got to go now I'll call you later.

God's Grace

Five months had passed and I was running through the airport to catch my flight to Florida and thinking how good it would be to see GG, Nicki, her new baby boy and all my friends.

I missed them but I had moved out the penthouse, bought a home in Buckhead and was making new friends. It's amazing how everything works out for the good of those who love the Lord. I found a new church and service is awesome.

I pray that Sherman has moved on and found what he couldn't in me.

As the plane touched down my stomach began to do flip flops. I would be staying with GG and Gregg was picking me up at the airport. I met him at baggage claim and he looked handsome as usual.

Hi gorgeous, how's everything?

He pulled me into his arms and gave me a big hug.

Everything is good and very good.

How is Gregg Jr?

He's handsome like his Papa.

We both laughed.

How long are you staying?

One week and then I have to get back. I don't need to be away from my desk too long.

We made it to the car and as we were leaving the airport I had to ask about Sherman. After the words left my mouth, I could have kicked myself.

I don't see much of him, only on Sunday's.

I must have looked funny because he went on to explain that Sherman had joined the church and was coming every Sunday. I just nodded my head. Gregg changed the subject fast and started talking about the baby and how his days and nights were mixed up. We arrived at their home in no time.

I walked in the house ahead of Gregg and saw the most precious sight I had ever seen, Nicki was nursing the most beautiful baby. I couldn't wait to hold him.

Oh Nicki he's beautiful.

She finished nursing and asked me if I wanted to hold him. I wasted no time washing my hands and reaching for my godson.

On Sunday he will be christened. Are you ready?

Girl I can't wait to spoil him.

We laughed as I held that bundle of joy.

So how is Atlanta? Nicki asked me.

Everything is going so good and I haven't had time to catch my breath. I bought a home and now I'm trying to decorate it. I joined a church and everyone there is nice.

So have you met any men? Girl you know I'm not looking for a man, the breakup with Sherman was bad enough on me and I'm just not ready for another relationship at this time.

Jackie you can't give up on love. I told Gregg everything and I mean everything and our relationship is so good now, no secrets and no drama. We have disagreements but what marriage doesn't? I never thought I would find a man as sweet and kind as he is. No I should say I didn't think that I deserved a good man. I messed up so much in the beginning that I thought God had forgotten all about me. Gregg makes me fill whole. He makes me feel loved and protected. I just can't thank God enough. I'm truly blessed and happy.

Well maybe one day I'll find that in a man but right now my work is my man and everything else and I'm content. You know when I left here I wanted Sherman to hurt as bad as I was hurting, I did a lot of blaming and cursing, *screaming and crying. But God's grace was sufficient and I got through it. You know the very thing that God is trying to protect us from. We run right to it, I'm ready to forgive him now and move on with my life. I know that now that I'm back in town I will run into him. Sometimes people have to love themselves before they can love others.*

Enough about this, how is motherhood.

I knew Jackie was trying to change the subject so I went along with it.

It's different when you have your own. You have to sleep when the baby sleeps and I'm always so tired but I'm happy and I wouldn't trade it for nothing in the world.

We talked for more than an hour and then Gregg stuck his head in the door and told us that dinner was ready.

We looked at each other and said in unison and said, *where has the time gone?*

I hadn't called GG to tell her I made it and I would see her in the morning so I made that call right away. I didn't want to worry her.

God Writes the End

Jackie woke up around two in the morning and couldn't get back to sleep so she went to the kitchen to get a glass of warm milk and found Gregg sitting at the table eating a piece of cake.

Come on in. Sit down and have a piece of cake. I was hoping that I would get a chance to talk to you alone. How are you really doing Jackie?

Really Gregg I'm doing good. See I thought I would have fallen apart by now, but through prayer and faith I'm still standing. God reigns over my life with power and majesty, He reigns over everything. Over my circumstance He's given me a second chance. I could have been broken and bitter but because He still reigns over me I'm ready to forgive and move forward with the rest of my life.

I just thought you should know that he still loves you and because of that love I've seen a big change in him. He comes to church every Sunday and he's truly repented for everything he's done to hurt anyone. I just think that he deserves a second chance with you.

In case you haven't noticed I don't live here anymore and I'm truly happy in Atlanta. I couldn't and I wouldn't pick up and move back here. I worked hard for the position I hold in the company and I don't want to give it up.

What if Sherman gave up his job and moved to Atlanta?

I don't think so. I could never trust him again.

So you are saying that even though God forgives us for our mistakes you cannot forgive another person for theirs?

No I'm saying I forgive him for hurting me but I will not put myself in a situation to be hurt again.

So you know that for the rest of your life no one will ever hurt you again?

God writes the end before your story is begun.

What does that mean?

It means that I see you and Sherman being happy together again. He made a mistake and because of it you are making him relive it over and over.

No that's not what I'm doing. I just don't want him anymore, that's all.

Jackie got up and began to head back to bed. Gregg stopped her in her tracks.

God is still in control of this situation.

She looked back at him with tears in her eyes.

And that is what frightens me so much.

Jackie laid in bed thinking about the conversation with Gregg and knew that she had never faced anything like this before. She began to pray to God for direction and for favor:

Lord, I thought I had this situation under control. Lord turn this mess I'm in into an awesome miracle, I know you can. God I know you never fail. I know you never lost a battle. Nothing is impossible with you. My back is against the wall, Lord please make a way out of no way for me. I need you to help me. There is nothing to hard for you Lord. Help me to make the right decision concerning Sherman and myself. This prayer is asked in your sweet son Jesus name. Amen.

Seasons

Jackie got back into bed and before she knew it the sun was coming through the window. She got up, checked on the baby who was still fast asleep, and went downstairs.

Nicki was sitting at the table drinking a glass of orange juice.

Hi.

Hi yourself. Did you sleep well?

I did.

Gregg already left for the day so what are you going to do today?

I'm going to see GG and by the time I'm finish visiting with her the crew should be here.

The doorbell rang before Jackie could finish speaking.

Oh that's mom. She's coming to stay with me and Gregg Jr for a while today.

Jackie got up to let in Mother Christine. She was surprised to see Sherman standing there instead.

She looked at him and couldn't think of a thing to say. Finally, she remembered her manners.

I'm sorry come in, was Nicki expecting you?

No I came to tell you welcome home and I hope that I get a chance to talk to you before you leave. My number is the same so if you can spare a little time I'll be grateful, and with that being said I'll leave and wait for your phone call.

He turned to leave, stopped and then turned back.

By the way Jackie, you're still looking good.

I watched him walk back to his car and drive off. I continued to stand there looking like a fool until Nicki called my name.

Who was at the door?

Sherman. He asked me for a few hours of my time if I could spare it, told me his number was the same and then walked away. I don't know what I expected but it wasn't that.

Nicki started laughing so hard that she had to sit down.

What's so funny?

If you can see the look on your face, you would laugh too.

Girl I'm so shocked. I didn't expect this new attitude from him.

I told you that he's changed. I think losing you was a major reason for his change. He's more responsible now, more focused and he's even stopped going out. Not only does he come to church but he's active in nearly every area. As a matter of fact, he's Gregg's armor bearer. God really changed him. I think that you should sit down with him and hear what he has to say to you.

Nicki I told you that I'm happy in Atlanta and with my church family.

I know but are you happy with your life as it is or are you missing something?

I just don't want to be hurt any more. Girl I'm telling you to give love another chance and I think you will be surprised at the outcome of it.

Have No Regrets

Jackie turned the key in her GG's door and before she could unlock it, she was in GG's arms.

I've missed you so much baby girl. I've been praying that you were happy and not grieving.

I'm happy GG, but most of all I'm happy to be home. How are you and what have you been up too?

You know your GG. I have been so busy with everybody and everything. Come in the kitchen and sit down tell me everything.

Jackie sat down at the table and told her GG everything that she had had done since leaving Florida.

They laughed at some of the things GG had been into since Jackie's departure and then they cried because they had missed each other so much.

Tell me if you think I should sit down and talk to Sherman or not.

Jackie what is it that you want? I've told you that you cannot tell your heart who to love. If you love him, you love him. Who are you trying to convince? Talk to him and see where it goes. Life is not always the way you see it. Sometimes you get hurt, and sometimes you're disappointed but you live through the good and the bad. No man is perfect no not one. We all fall short. The only thing for certain is life and death. We make mistakes, correct them if we can and move on with life. For most of my life I've been happy with the choices I've made and when I made a mistake I asked for forgiveness and moved on. I've loved, laughed, and cried but as you can see I'm still living and doing the best that I can. I'm happy baby and I have no regrets to look back on and wish that I had done something different. So I'm telling you to trust God and follow your heart.

Thank you GG this is why I love you so much!

Sherman was headed to Gregg's house for the second time today, but this time was different, he would be seeing Jackie. He tried to think of something witty to say but all he knew was that this would be the only chance to convince her that he loved her and wanted her as his wife.

He began to pray:

God, I'm standing on your word knowing that you are a man who cannot lie. You said that I could ask anything of you in your son Jesus name and you would give it to me. I'm standing in need of your mercy and grace right now. If it's in your will, not mine, I ask you to order my steps and bridle my tongue to what I want to say and give me words of wisdom and knowledge to convey to Jackie. Lord I love you and I come into agreement with your word. Strengthen me and please help me to say the right things in your sweet name I ask this, Amen.

S tanding in the window hiding behind the curtains Jackie watched as Sherman drove up the driveway. Her heart was racing like a wild horse. Her throat was getting dry as she watched him exit the car and walk to the door.

Her mind went back to all the good things she had admired about him. His smile could and almost had melted her panties off plenty of nights on his couch. His kisses were so smooth and his touch was hypnotic.

Jackie didn't know what to do, run away or answer the door.

Gregg and Nicki had retired to the bedroom after dinner and had left me to entertain Sherman alone. They both had agreed this was my call and they wouldn't interfere. I was lost in the past and now here was Sherman knocking at the door offering me a future.

I opened the door and invited him in.

You look beautiful.

He handed me flowers.

Come in and have a seat while I put these in water. They are beautiful by the way. Thank you.

You are beautiful.

And I realized he was right behind me.

One look in his eyes and I was in his arms, kissing his lips and putting my hands all over his magnificent body. I pulled back first and apologized for had just happened.

No don't apologize. I needed to know that at least you still found me desirable. Look Jackie I am going to be honest with you. I didn't mean for any of the things that happened to hurt you. I love you and I was not thinking when I went out on that date. I know it was wrong and I'm asking now for your forgiveness. I've changed in so many ways. I want to give you the world! I've missed you so much. I need you so much and I give you my word that nothing will ever make me act so irresponsible again. Give me another chance to love you.

Jackie heard Sherman speaking and her hard heart was melting with every word he spoke. When he got on his knees and pulled out a ring, she knew that her answer would be yes. He proposed to her a second time within a year and this time, she said yes.

Sherman kissed Jackie and pulled her into his arms and she knew then that in his arms was where she belonged.

They talked over into the night and when Jackie looked at the clock it was past two so she told him he had to go.

That night before she went to bed, Jackie talked to God to make sure she hadn't made another mistake that would cost her dearly.

Go Through To Get To

J ackie got up early to fix breakfast for everyone. Nicki stepped in the kitchen with a smile on her face.

Do I hear wedding bells?

Yes, you do, but I haven't worked out all the details yet. We couldn't decide if he was moving to Atlanta or I was moving back home. We are getting married. I can't believe that I said yes. I just decided to forgive him and move on I didn't even think about it, now I'm beginning to have second thoughts Nicki what am I doing?

You are doing what your heart says is right. Forgiving and marrying the man that you love. It's going to work out in your favor trust and believe.

G regg and Sherman were having breakfast at the diner across from Sherman's office and talking about what happened last night.

I will follow her to the moon and back. I love her so much.

So you have made your mind up to leave here and move to Atlanta?

Yes, I don't want her to pick up and move back here. I'll be good in Atlanta.

Does she know this?

No but I want to make her happy and she said that she was happy in Atlanta.

I'm going to miss you. You know how hard it is for a pastor to find an honest and good right hand man. What am I going to do without you?

I'm here for the next six months and by then we will have found the right man for you, I have one in mind now. I need to talk with him and then I will set up a meeting with the two of you. How does that sound?

Man you are working hard to get things right.

I know. Let me get busy and I'll talk to you later.

Sherman walked back to his office and called Pastor Willis and set up a meeting with him at the church around three.

At three, Sherman was walking into Pastor's office.

The two men shook hands and got down to business. After they talked about Sherman's impending move to

Atlanta, they then began discussing Kenny as Gregg's new armor bearer.

Kenny is single, but he has never been in trouble, he's a deacon in good standing, a strong man of God and an overall good man. I think he will be great for Gregg.

Pastor Willis agreed with Sherman.

Let me get him on the phone and see if he's interested.

Sherman walked around the spacious office while Pastor and Kenny talked. Pastor hung up the phone, looked at me and nodded his head in agreement.

He's willing to meet with us and talk about it. He's not making promises though. Sometimes when God is moving in our lives we don't see it and we are people who like to see things happening rather than believe it can happen. So we let God deal with that. I wanted to tell you that although I'm not proud of what you did I'm proud of how you handled yourself through it. You became a man in the process of your struggles and I'm so proud of you. We sometimes have to go through to get to. Now I want to know what your plans are after you get to Atlanta.

Pastor thank you for being in my corner all these years. I am going to become a member of Jackie's church and do what I can there.

You know son, God has a calling on your life.

I don't think he wants me to preach 'cause I'm just barely getting it right with my life.

Pastor gave me a look and then changed the subject. We talked a while longer and then I left to meet Jackie for an early dinner. After dinner she and I went to my mother's home for dessert and to tell her the news together.

Mom was so happy and a little sad to know that I would be leaving in six months but she gave her blessings. Uncle Dale gave his blessings also.

I dropped Jackie at Nicki's house and went home.

The next morning I began the process of finding an office in Atlanta and building my clientele there. God was blessing me because I found a nice office in Buckhead not too far from Jackie's home and I even started a new webpage for my business.

I put everything on the website and people began to post on my page instantly. I was looking for a secretary, an office manager and someone to answer the phones. I started taking calls and scheduling interviews.

Around five I had finished all I could for the day. I couldn't wait to be married to Jackie I was going to be a great husband.

Eight Months Later ...

G regg and Nicki were relaxing in the living room when someone rang their doorbell.

Who could that be? Gregg, are you expecting someone?

No I'm not. Gregg opened the door and Rhonda and Kenny were standing there.

Is anything wrong at the church? Gregg asked.

No we just wanted to talk to you and Nicki for a second. Kenny said.

Come on in don't just stand there. Nicki insisted.

We were all seated and looking at each other. Finally Gregg said, *Well we're listening.*

Rhonda looked nervous and Kenny cleared his throat and began to speak.

I don't know where to start, but to make a long story short, Rhonda and I came over so that could ask you Pastor Gregg not only for your sister's hand in marriage but also for your blessings. I know that you might think that this is all of a sudden but fact of the matter is I've been courting Rhonda since the first week she joined the church.

Gregg and Nicki's mouth fell open and then we all burst out laughing.

Everything is going on at once. Gregg said. And then he got serious.

Rhonda you are the only sister I have in this world and I don't want to see you hurt. Are you sure Kenny is the one that you love and are you sure that you're ready for marriage?

Gregg, I'm so in love with this man. He makes me laugh. He makes me happy and I couldn't live without him. So big brother you might as well give your blessings because with or without it I'm marrying this man!

We all laughed again and gave each other hugs.

Gregg blessed them and hugged the both of them one more time.

Welcome to the family Kenny.

Lying in bed that night, Gregg looked at Nicki and made his thoughts known to her.

Who knew Rhonda and Kenny were seeing each other?

I certainly didn't, I never even saw them talking to one another let along dating.

It looks like I have a new armor bearer and a brother-in-law all rolled up in one.

I can't wait to see if Sherman knew.

Later that morning, Gregg strolled into Sherman's office. Sherman looked up with some apprehension.

Hey, Gregg. What's up with you?

Did you know that Kenny and Rhonda were dating?

Yea man everybody knew that.

What? They came over last night and asked for my blessings and wanted to let me know that they were getting married. It blew my mind.

You gave it I hope?

Yes of course I did, I want my sister to be happy, and she says Kenny does that.

Good because you can be a bit over protective.

What? Man you are tripping.

Yea right! Anyway, I'm glad you stopped by because I was wondering if you would fly to Atlanta with me to finalize all my plans. I'm so excited, my business is up and running smoothly in Atlanta, I found the perfect office manager and we've found the perfect home, now I'm just waiting to take my place as Jackie's husband.

It turned out ok didn't it?

Yes it did! God did that! All in due Season!

To everything there is a season,

And a time to every purpose under the heaven:

A time to be born, and a time to die:

A time to plant, and a time to pluck up

That which is planted:

A time to kill, and a time to heal;

A time to break down, and a time to build up;

A time to weep, and a time to laugh;

A time to mourn, and a time to dance;

A time to cast away stone,

And a time to embrace, and a time

To refrain from embracing;

A time to get, and a time to lose;

A time to keep, and a time to cast away;

A time to rend, and a time to sew;

A time to keep silence, and a time to speak;

A time to love, and a time to hate;

A time of war, and a time of peace.

Ecclesiastes 3:1-8

About the Author

Author Tina Melson is a mom of four, grandmother of four and great-grandmother of one. After working in the school system for more years than she can count, she wanted to write.

Writing has always been her passion and now that she's retired she has more time to dedicate to the craft.

Tina finds that writing is therapeutic and hopes that her labor of love will not only entertain you but help you find closure to some seasons in your life!

Our God is a God of the unexpected!

Secrets

The Sequel to *Seasons*

The Plan

How did I end up in this situation? I've asked myself this question over and over again in the last few days. All I can come up with are more questions: *How in the world am I going to come out of this? Why didn't I think before I acted?*

I remember my mother's words now so many years after she has passed away, "*You are going to get yourself into a world of trouble one day by thinking that the world owes you something,*" she'd said. "*You had better learn to think with the right head that God gave you.*" I can still hear her voice as if she were standing right here next to me.

I've always thought that I was God's gift to women. Now that I've been hit with this information, I'm not so sure anymore. As head Deacon of one of the largest churches in Atlanta, I am in for the fight of my life. I never intended for things to get so out of hand.

James didn't think to ask God for help because to him it was always about what James wanted and not about what he needed. And at this moment he needed God.

Pacing around his spacious den, he stopped to look out at the beauty of his yard and what he thought that he had created all by himself. He was a very proud man and very private.

He began to pace again and tried to figure out just where he had went wrong. He remembered feeling so excited that day. After he had gotten off work, he showered and took longer than usual to get dressed. He accessed his generous wardrobe and picked out one of his best suites and worried a few minutes longer than necessary over the color shirt and tie he would wear. But in the end he chose a midnight blue shirt with a matching tie and was satisfied with his choice.

As he backed out of his driveway he looked in the rearview mirror at his big beautiful home and was puffed up with pride at all he had accomplished. Smiling to himself he gunned the motor of his new jaguar and headed off for a night of fun and relaxation. But he what he hadn't known was that God had a plan for his life.

The Butterfly Typeface Publishing

The Butterfly Typeface is full service professional writing, editing and publishing company. Our goal is to 'spread the message' of inspiration, imagination and intrigue in all that we do. Whether you hire us to edit, ghostwrite, publish (books & magazines) or web design, you can be guaranteed exemplary customer service, fairness and quality. Our vision, under God's leadership, is to serve and assist in the healing of the heart, mind and soul of *all* people we encounter with integrity, intentional influence and positive purpose.

"We make good GREAT!"

Iris M Williams – Owner
PO Box 56193
Little Rock Arkansas
501.681.0080

www.thebutterflytypeface.com

butterflytypeface.imw@gmail.com